D1255868

CHURCH AND SCHOOL

SOCIAL RESEARCH SERIES

General Editor: T. S. Simey

Other titles in this Series:

Joan Brothers

Church and School

WITHDRAWN

A STUDY OF THE IMPACT
OF EDUCATION ON RELIGION

Social Research Series

LIVERPOOL UNIVERSITY PRESS 1964

LIVERPOOL UNIVERSITY PRESS

123 Grove Street · Liverpool 7

PRINTED AND BOUND IN ENGLAND BY HAZELL WATSON AND VINEY LTD
AYLESBURY, BUCKS

PREFACE

THE present book is an important contribution to the sociology of religion, as it enlarges the frontiers of the subject so as to include aspects of human conduct which are, quite clearly, both religious and social. It is not merely sociographic or demographic in the sense that it seeks to describe the social characteristics of a population, class or group defined by attitudes to religion, as is the case with religious sociology; such studies may have a value of their own to those who seek to acquire data that are significant for the purpose of extending the influence of a church or other religious organization, but this is not the primary concern in sociological research. In contrast, Dr Brothers's work is intended to be an objective study of religion and religious institutions; it is primarily directed towards an understanding of the interaction between the organization, structure, and activities of a church and those of the wider society in which it is placed. Whilst her approach is that of an empirical sociologist, she assumes that the objectives of her study, as such, must be limited to the natural and the observable, and that as religion transcends these boundaries, ultimate spiritual realities cannot be subjected to this kind of analysis. These assumptions do not imply, however, that her work is only concerned with the superficial, or that its value is low. She would also assert that what she has studied is a very important part of God's creation, providing as it does the context within which the religious life is led, and the form which gives it outward shape. As the influence of both of these on the religious life itself must be strong, regard must be had to them as much by the theologian as the sociologist.

Studies in the sociology of religion of this kind, therefore, extend sociological analysis into a new area of social experience. In *Priests and People*, an earlier volume in this series, Dr Conor Ward has shown how the internal social organization of a parish interlocked with that of the larger religious society of the archdiocese, on the one hand, and with the secular society of the neighbourhood, on the other. His analysis was directed, for instance, to a fuller understanding of the role of the priest within the parish, and the structure of diocesan organizations. Dr Brothers takes this method of approach a stage further. She is concerned with the double problem which arises when changes in the organization of the civic community lead to similar changes in the social structure of the parish; this has a direct impact on the social life and personal experiences of Catholics, and this, again, has changed the social context within which the

Church has to work. The final result is that a new kind of religious life has emerged for the persons affected. Whilst religion itself may be undisturbed, Dr Brothers has shown that a new social situation has arisen, incorporating changes of a revolutionary order, to which the Church must give the most careful and most urgent consideration in matters not only of church organization but of theological thought as well.

The theoretical significance and practical importance of Dr Brothers's book are therefore correspondingly great. Her argument stands on the outer frontiers of knowledge in which both scientific enquiry and theological understanding have to be employed simultaneously in the analysis of an extremely complex series of events. In so far as her work shows how scientific research can be carried out so as to bridge the intellectual gulf between man's life in the natural world and his existence as a spiritual being, which has of late become increasingly hard to cross, her achievement extends far beyond the limits of the social sciences. Her book may well come as a shock to those who believe that the basis of sociological work must be positivist, and that sociology can only exist as a science if it is assumed that there is no reality which its own categories of comprehension cannot understand.

The author wishes to express her thanks to all those who have helped her to carry out the research on which this book is based, and in the analysis of the material and the presentation of the argument embodied in it. She is especially indebted to Dr John Mays, Miss Elizabeth Gittus and Dr Charles Vereker in this regard. Professor E. F. O'Doherty gave her invaluable help by his most constructive criticism, in particular by discussing with her the implications of her findings from both the theological and sociological points of view. Most of all, however, her gratitude must be acknowledged to all those with whom the research brought her into contact, whose interest and encouragement were decisive in enabling her to complete what was at times a most worrying and exhausting venture. This interest was expressed with a patent sincerity, and a frankness which was often as courageous as it was painstaking. If this book is found to deal with any of the more urgent issues of modern life, therefore, that must ultimately be attributed to the clergy, teachers, and former grammar school pupils who co-operated so generously in its compilation. Dr Brothers hopes that they may find in its publication some reward for their trouble.

T. S. SIMEY,

Department of Social Science,
The University, Liverpool.

CONTENTS

CONTENTS

Chapter 1

INTRODUCTION

ALTHOUGH the term 'social change' has become a cliché in the social sciences, the literature of the subject contains little on the empirical level which describes and explains the factors involved in the processes while these are actually taking place. In particular, the consequences of planned change have been largely neglected. It has, indeed, been pointed out recently that 'for one reason or another, sociologists have been prone to ignore the most striking characteristics of modern society—rapid change, and intelligent and responsible attempts to guide or stimulate change in such a way as to lead to better conditions of life.'[1]

While experiments concerning change are common in the field of social psychology or in an industrial setting,[2] there seems to be room for research into what happens when more general changes are taking place within society itself. Many changes in our society today do not represent spontaneous developments in social life. They are deliberate innovations, designed to alter some aspects of behaviour or institutions. Our educational system may be described as a crucial experiment of this kind. Yet in spite of its central influence in shaping society, remarkably little is known about the way it may introduce social change. Ironically, much of the research which has been carried out in this country reveals how little change education has produced.[3] But a great deal of this work has been focused upon the social class system, and it seems worthwhile considering how other aspects of our society may be affected through innovations in the sphere of education.

This study sets out to show how changes in the educational system have affected religious attitudes and institutions; to be precise, it deals with the consequences which current educational policy is having for the social organization of Roman Catholicism in Liverpool.

Education and Social Change

The Education Act of 1944 was designed to bring about far-reaching

1. T. S. Simey, 'The Relevance of Sociology to the Training of Teachers and Social Workers', *The Sociological Review Monograph No. 4* (July, 1961), p. 22.
2. E.g. E. Jaques, *The Changing Culture of a Factory*, London, 1951. Reprinted 1957.
3. Some evidence to the contrary is contained in *15–18* (commonly referred to as the Crowther Report), H.M.S.O., London, 1959.

changes in the educational system of Great Britain. Research into its consequences makes it increasingly plain, however, that in some spheres of society the amount of social change which it is producing is less than many would wish. Floud, Halsey and Martin, for instance, have shown that it is easier for a child from a middle class family to be selected for a grammar school education. Although more children from working class homes are now attending grammar schools, ability is not the only factor; social class is still a very important determinant in selection for secondary education.[1] The Central Advisory Council for Education has produced similarly disquieting reports, especially *15–18* and *Early Leaving*; the latter, for instance, reveals that the age of school leaving is related to social factors rather than to educational ability.[2] In a more specific context, in a recent study of schools in central Liverpool, Dr. Mays has shown how the impact of educational change in this area is much smaller than one might have expected.[3] So there is not much evidence as yet from which one can conclude that the 1944 Education Act is producing a society which is radically different from that which was previously in existence.

However, much of the work undertaken so far on the consequences of the 1944 Education Act has been directed towards the social class system.[4] How the educational system has affected other aspects of society remains to be considered. A new educational policy, that of providing a secondary education for all children without the payment of fees, might be expected to introduce changes into many spheres of the social structure of Britain. Moreover, with our present ignorance of social variables, it is more than likely that some of the effects of these educational innovations will not have been intended. Although the present study is concerned to some extent with social stratification, its primary aim is to consider how changes are brought about in religious groupings, and in particular to discover how the social organization of a religious group may be altered, both consciously and in an unintended direction, as a result of educational

1. J. E. Floud (Ed.), A. H. Halsey, F. M. Martin, *Social Class and Educational Opportunity*, London, 1956. An interesting comparison can be found in M. Matthijssen, 'Onderwijs en sociaal milieu in Zuid Limburg', *Social Compass*, V, 4, 150–74. This Dutch inquiry into secondary education reveals that, in the area considered, mental ability was not the decisive factor in secondary education, but the social class to which one belonged was more important; the writer concludes that the chances of children from the working class becoming socially mobile are still comparatively slight.

2. *Early Leaving*, H.M.S.O., London, 1954.

3. J. B. Mays, *Education and the Urban Child*, Liverpool University Press, 1962.

4. See, for instance, the extremely interesting and provocative study carried out by B. Jackson and D. Marsden, *Education and the Working Class*, London, 1962.

change. Studying as it does the relationship between religious values, behaviour and institutions with regard to Roman Catholicism in Liverpool, the investigation lies more properly in the sphere of the sociology of religion than that of education or social stratification.

The 1944 Education Act has brought with it many changes which have influenced the social structure of the Catholic Church in Britain. It was essential, therefore, to define the precise area of investigation more narrowly. The extension of grammar school education and its social consequences seemed to offer the most fruitful field for inquiry. Education and occupation are closely related in Britain today. Although social mobility may be achieved through other factors, such as large increases in earnings, it is usually education which enables people to become mobile.[1] Hence, one of the most important aspects of social change lies in the extension of grammar school education to a wider section of society. The time, moreover, was opportune for such an inquiry. Though the 1944 Education Act was not responsible for introducing grammar school education, it accelerated, through the abolition of fees, the process of expansion which had already begun. Thus, the phenomenon of Catholic children attending grammar schools was by no means new, but it had grown considerably in the immediate past. An examination of it thus necessarily led to the study of social change while it was actually taking place.

A further inducement to undertake a study of this kind arose from the fact that a considerable amount of material which could be used in it was already available. In the educational sphere, an increasing number of studies are appearing which deal with the question of entrance to a grammar school and the effects of this form of education.[2] Moreover, relevant material was also available in the sociology of religion, for a survey of a Liverpool parish had been completed in 1959 which described the social organization of the general body of Catholics.[3] This study, carried out by Dr. Ward, was not specifically related to change, but it was directly helpful in so far as it did much to sketch in the background within which this present research was carried out.

There was another reason, too, why this subject was selected for research. The writer had herself attended a Liverpool Catholic grammar school, and so was aware from personal experience what this might entail for an individual. She wanted to discover how far her own impressions and opinions could be said to fit into a general

1. See D. V. Glass (Ed.), *Social Mobility in Britain*, London, 1954, *passim*.
2. E.g. Brother Gregory, 'The Dual System and the Performance of Children in an 11+ Examination, *The Sociological Review*, N.S., VI, 1 (1958), 25–36.
3. C. K. Ward, *Priests and People*, Liverpool University Press, 1961.

pattern. Knowing intimately many others involved in this situation made her conscious of how different the attitudes of the former pupils of Catholic grammar schools were from those of the parishioners of St. Catherine's in Dr. Ward's study. In addition to the intrinsic interest which the study of religious behaviour and attitudes had for the writer, it seemed that a knowledge of the situation gained from having lived within the Catholic community all her life would be an advantage in understanding how the processes of change were affecting the social structure and organization of Roman Catholicism.

But this interest was not simply the result of personal involvement. Although what is called 'grammar school education' differs from place to place, and discussion of any of it must be confined to a fairly narrowly defined region, wider issues always arise and are far-reaching. It is not only Catholics in Liverpool who are becoming socially mobile in an urban and industrialized society. The general features of the situation are to be found in many parts of the world. Immigrants in countries such as the United States have for many years been settling into a society which is new to them, and are emerging from the working class in the same way as people interviewed in this investigation. And in many other countries throughout the world the rise of the middle classes comes as a consequence of rapidly expanding economies. It is not enough to cite the evidence which indicates that the higher the standard of his education, the more likely a Catholic is to fulfil his duties of church attendance, an issue discussed later in this chapter. There is more to the life of a Christian than attending church. We need more research to tell us how this section of people, emerging as they are into a new social world, understand their religious beliefs, and how they relate them to the new society in which they live, and the old one which they leave. We have yet to discover how their values affect their behaviour, and indeed, what motivates the behaviour itself. There are so many issues which remain to be tackled. In the meantime, it is only by the careful and detailed consideration of the behaviour and ideas of small sections of people that advances can be made in understanding what happens to the religious life of those who are becoming socially mobile.

The writer, then, was motivated not by academic aims alone, or even in the last analysis, by any academic aims at all, but chiefly by the desire to consider in practical terms topics which are of crucial importance in the Christian way of living. The excitement and pressures of change in the world today are reflected in the formal policies of the Roman Catholic Church as well as in the lives of the members. The development of the theology of the laity is a conspicuous example of how changing social structures have made it necessary to re-open issues that were thought to be closed many years ago, but it now appears that this was so only in ways adapted to the needs of earlier generations. This study reveals some of the new problems with which a changing society confronts the Church. It was not so long ago, for instance, that an English Catholic could not attend a university in his own country. Now the numbers of Catholic students in British universities are increasing at a rapid rate.[1] The attempts to cope with the religious needs of such people are described in this book. Sometimes, however, social changes are not so easily discerned. Attitudes towards religion fall into this category. A parish priest, for instance, may suspect that certain of his parishioners think differently from their parents, but he may be uncertain of the direction of their thoughts. The time seems opportune to step back from the situation, to stop for a while to attempt a sociological analysis of the changes which are being brought about in the social structure of Roman Catholicism in Liverpool, and how they in their turn are affecting the organization of the Church. There is, too, the other side of the coin, the influence of the Church upon the same events, to consider.

New Attitudes Towards Education

In the last fifteen or more years, the number of places in Catholic grammar schools in Liverpool, as elsewhere, has grown considerably, partly through expanding the intake of new pupils, and partly by building new schools or altering the status of others to bring them to the level of grammar schools.[2] Whether or not this increasing attention given to grammar schools by the Catholic Church in Liverpool can be directly attributed to the 1944 Education Act is a difficult question to answer. It might perhaps be more correctly described as being the result of social attitudes produced in part by the Act. The population as a whole is becoming more conscious of the social and economic advantages to be derived from a grammar school education. The prestige attached to going to a grammar school is now such that it has become customary for a child to be considered as having 'failed' the selection examination if he is not assigned a place in such a school. In this way, the status which such a child is expected to

1. See *Catholics in the Universities: the Next Decade*, Newman Demographic Survey, London, 1960.
2. The Reports of the Education Committee of the City Council, Liverpool, give statistics of children in Catholic grammar schools over the years. But since some Catholic children were in non-Catholic grammar schools, these figures do not refer to the total number of Catholic children receiving a grammar school education. For more general statistics with relation to Catholics, see *Catholic Education. A Handbook*, Catholic Educational Council for England and Wales, London, 1960–61. See especially, A. E. C. W. Spencer, 'The Post-War Growth of the Catholic Child Population of England and Wales', pp. 18–29.

achieve later in life might almost be described as being anticipated at the age of eleven.

Catholics have shared this awareness of the advantages of grammar school education. There has been a growing stress on the fact that if the ideal of educating Catholic children in Catholic schools is to be a reality and if, at the same time, Catholics are to maintain a place in the community in proportion to their numbers, more Catholic grammar school places must be made available. Dr. Heenan, former Archbishop of Liverpool, for instance, has spoken publicly of the shortage of Catholic grammar schools in Liverpool.[1] Many of the Liverpool parishioners described by Dr. Ward apparently shared this consciousness of the present shortage of Catholic grammar school places.[2] Where Catholics are few in number, Catholic children sometimes attend local authority schools, especially grammar schools. But in Liverpool, the size of the Catholic population makes it possible for many Catholic schools to be maintained; these include ten secondary schools in the city itself, which, although differing in their relationship with the Ministry of Education (a matter which is discussed in Chapter 5), may be termed grammar schools. As a result, it is rare for Catholics in Liverpool to receive from the Archbishop the permission which is necessary before their children may be sent to non-Catholic schools, although a few, especially boys, have been allowed to attend local authority grammar schools because of the shortage of places in Catholic grammar schools.[3]

Catholicism in Liverpool

This study is concerned with the impact made upon the social organization of Catholicism by new attitudes towards education. It also deals with the phenomenon of growing numbers of Catholic children attending grammar schools. Before the effects of such changes in the educational pattern can be considered, however, it is essential to give some attention to the ways in which members of the Catholic Church in Liverpool were grouped together in the past. Fortunately, a good deal of information on this is already available from contemporary sociological accounts as well as from historical sources.

1. For example, his address at a prizegiving ceremony of one of the grammar schools. Cited in *The Catholic Herald*, 13th December, 1957.
2. *Op. cit.*, pp. 97–8.
3. It is realized, of course, that some Catholic children attend local authority schools without permission. But the religious sanctions against sending a child to a non-Catholic school without permission are strong. To do so involves a serious break from the norms of the group. The attitudes of the parents, then, are likely to be different from those of the ordinary body of Catholics. Those who attend local authority grammar schools, with or without permission, are omitted from the present study because the investigation is concerned with the effects of attending a *Catholic* grammar school.

The history of the neighbourhoods which now form part of the city of Liverpool reveals the strength of recusancy during times of persecution, especially amongst certain families.[1] Yet in spite of the influence such people have had in shaping English Catholicism, the Church in Liverpool today is more usually associated with the influx of immigrants from Ireland in the eighteenth and nineteenth centuries.[2] Liverpool Catholics probably think far more readily of Irish traditions than they do of those which were once so strong in the area[3]. Much of the present social system and the attitudes surrounding it are most easily intelligible in the light of the events of the last two centuries.[4] The immigrants brought with them the traditional devotion of the Irish to their priesthood (a phenomenon which can again be understood in its historical context), and this has been a factor of tremendous importance in the cultural development of Catholicism in the city. Finding themselves in a religious and social minority, the loyalty of these immigrants to their group grew easily.[5] Dr. Mays describes in vivid terms the ways in which adversity drew them together; having referred to the feelings of solidarity which developed during the cholera epidemic of 1847, he goes on to say:

Being a minority group in a land officially Protestant must have strengthened these ties which an awareness of their common Irish descent further emphasised. Their history as a Liverpool community has been one of constant adversity, which, we know, is a powerful creator of a corporate spirit. The immigrants were driven to these shores by the threat of starvation; they were forced to inhabit the worst dwellings in the poorest parts of the city; they have lived in comparative poverty ever since and grown accustomed to casual employment, low wages and social inferiority. Such conditions could not fail to have fostered some feelings of resentment and bitterness and other symptoms familiarly associated with out-groups in similar

1. See, for example, R. J. Stonor, *Liverpool's Hidden Story*, Billinge, Lancashire, 1957.
2. See J. V. Hickey, *The Irish Rural Immigrant and British Urban Society*, Newman Demographic Survey, London, 1960, especially Section III, pp. 23–46. See also, J. A. Jackson, 'The Irish in Britain', *The Sociological Review*, N.S., X, 1 (1962), 5–16.
3. In this connection, the names of Liverpool parishes offer interesting reading. While many bear the names of saints widely popular in the Catholic Church, such as St. Anthony of Padua and St. Francis of Assisi, it is significant that several are dedicated to Irish saints, such as Malachy, Brigid, and Patrick, rather than to English saints. Two newly opened parishes bear the names of Irish saints, too, Finbar and Brendan. A different approach, however, is being introduced in the naming of the new inter-parochial schools. Several are named after English men and women put to death in the reign of Elizabeth I. For instance, one in the process of being built is bearing the name of Blessed Margaret Clitherow, who was put to death at York. Another, which was built several years ago, is called after Blessed John Almond, a priest who was born about 1577 not far from the place where the school now stands.
4. See, for instance, T. Burke, *Catholic History of Liverpool*, Liverpool, 1910.
5. M. B. Simey, *Charitable Effort in Liverpool in the Nineteenth Century*, Liverpool University Press, 1951, p. 16.

situations. In so far as the Irish Catholics have clung to their traditional culture, they have consciously resisted assimilation by the wider community.[1]

The Parish

It is also necessary to pay careful attention to the stress placed by the priests upon the importance of the parish as a focal point, not only because of the spiritual allegiances thus created, but also for the social loyalties that accompanied them. It is as well to remember in this context that both pastor and the faithful had known the rural community from which the concept of the parish as a social group has derived so much strength. Obviously, the parochial schools played an important part in establishing and maintaining solidarity amongst parishioners.[2] They were—and are—not merely a way of educating children and a means whereby young Catholics grow to know one another. They represent to the Catholics certain ideals which they treasure and are ready to defend. From the beginning, these schools have been surrounded by controversy, and they are still very much a social and political issue.[3] The building of them has involved considerable financial sacrifices, and at the present time many parishes are burdened by heavy debts to pay for them. The pride which has gone into maintaining these schools is thus understandable. Every visit paid to parochial schools during the fieldwork for this research evoked detailed accounts of how they were built and financed, and the old shabby buildings which had little to commend them to the visitor were described with as much enthusiasm as the newer ones. The addition of such a small thing as a partition was apparently a matter of importance and involved care in handling regulations. It seemed all were immensely conscious of their status as Catholic schools.

In spite of pressures towards social change, it appears that much of the loyalty and traditional groupings of Catholics around the parish still persists today. From Dr. Mays's account of the south dockland area of Liverpool, it would seem that the structure of the parish, formed on a territorial basis, is still an important reference group for Catholics.[4] In a region where much of the social life, including that centred on the schools, recreation and sometimes even work, is a

1. J. B. Mays, *Growing Up in the City. A Study of Juvenile Delinquency in an Urban Neighbourhood*, Liverpool University Press, second impression, 1956, p. 57.

2. See Ward, *op. cit.*, pp. 92 *et seq.* See also J. Fichter, *The Parochial School. A Sociological Study*, University of Notre Dame Press, 1958.

3. See B. D. White, *A History of the Corporation of Liverpool, 1835–1914*, Liverpool, 1951, pp. 141 *et seq.*, and J. Murphy, *The Religious Problem in English Education. The Crucial Experiment* Liverpool University Press, 1959.

4. *Op. cit.*, pp. 56 *et seq.*

neighbourhood affair, and where many people tend to remain nearby after marriage, the concept of a social grouping based on the territorial parish is not an administrative and legal device, but one which describes a living community founded upon a social reality. It might almost be said that in such areas being 'a good Catholic' is synonymous with being 'a good parishioner'; that is, someone who is loyal to the parish and takes an active part in parochial affairs.

Another factor emerging with clarity from Dr. Mays's study is the importance of the role of the parish priest as a social leader.[1] His realm is far from being confined to the religious sphere. The dominance of the parish priest in the lives of Catholics is also emphasized by Dr. Ward in describing the life of a Liverpool parish.[2] The former Archbishop of Liverpool commented recently in a pastoral letter on the way in which newspaper reporters visiting the city were amazed at the devotion of Liverpool Catholics to their priests: 'What they saw fascinated them, and what they found most striking was the bond between priest and people.'[3]

In analyzing the ways in which a Liverpool parish was operating, Dr. Ward presents a great deal of material which is relevant to the present inquiry. Particular attention was given in his study to the extent to which the parishioners' lives were influenced by the parish. While the account makes it clear that St. Catherine's parish was active in many ways, nevertheless, it is apparent from the results that, in the urban setting of Liverpool, the social aspects of the parochial system are adapting with difficulty to social change. In fact, there were occasions in the life of St. Catherine's parish which could be interpreted as evidence of resistance to change.[4] One reviewer, himself a Liverpool parish priest, drawing his own conclusions from the findings, went so far as to say:

In fact, St. Catherine's is a nineteenth century parish, doing very well indeed, but like many of the Church's institutions in England, it hasn't been brought into the twentieth century.[5]

The present inquiry sets out from this description of the parish's laboured adaptation to change. St. Catherine's parish had yet to face the problem of coping with large numbers of parishioners who had attended grammar schools; it was largely homogeneous in social structure, its population being predominantly working class. This

1. *Ibid.*, pp. 54 *et seq.*   2. *Ibid.*, pp. 58 *et seq.*
3. The Most Reverend John Carmel Heenan in his *Pastoral Letter and Report on the Priests' Training Fund*, Lent, 1961.
4. See, for instance, the situation with regard to the instructing of Catholic children in non-Catholic schools, Ward, *op. cit.*, pp. 93–4.
5. Benet Innes, in *The Universe*, 7th July, 1961.

present study was interested in discovering, amongst other things, to what extent the most important social grouping of the Catholic Church, the territorial parish, can absorb the consequences of further social change. How do young Catholics who have attended grammar schools perceive this social institution? Do they still identify it with Catholicism? Or do they regard the parish as being part of a cultural way of living from which their education and social status have removed them? Is the parish priest their 'moral mentor', as Dr. Mays reports that he is for Catholics in the south dockland areas?[1]

The practical relevance of these questions to the situation may be seen more clearly if it is pointed out that however many criticisms may be levelled against it at the present time, the parish is still the basic ecclesiastical unit of the Catholic Church. While the legal status of the parish is clearly defined in Canon Law,[2] and the juridical authority of the parish priest is established with some exactitude in it, other aspects of the parish are more elusive. Around the administrative and legal functions of the parish, various kinds of social groupings have developed in a variety of historical contexts. The precise nature of these differs from one place to another. As a result, there is some difficulty in achieving a generally acceptable definition of the parish as a social institution. In spite of a series of meetings in Brussels early in 1962, when a group of prominent theologians attempted to define its function as an ecclesiastical unit,[3] at the Seventh International Conference on the Sociology of Religion, held in Germany in the summer of the same year, it still proved difficult to arrive at a final conclusion in this matter, the greatest obstacle being the theological definition of the parish.[4] Differences in the social aspects of parochial organizations made agreement on the essential nature of the parish very hard to achieve.

For the present purposes, it is important to remember that the social life of the Catholic parish has taken a variety of forms throughout the world. While certain countries have developed groupings which are similar in some respects, as in the case of the North American and English type, for example,[5] differences in concept and practice make it difficult to classify them. Thus the parochial communities in Liverpool represent only one of the many varieties that exist in the modern world.[6]

1. *Op. cit.*, p. 58.
2. *Codex Iuris Canonici*, Vatican City, 1947; see especially Canon 216. Also P. M. Hannan, 'The Development of the Form of the Modern Parish', in C. J. Nuesse and T. J. Harte, *The Sociology of the Parish*, Milwaukee, 1951.
3. 'Mission et Paroisse', *La Revue Nouvelle*, XXXV, 6 (1962), 579–92.
4. Acts of the Seventh International Conference on the Sociology of Religion.
5. See J. H. Fichter, *Southern Parish, Volume I. Dynamics of a City Church*, Chicago, 1951, and J. B. Schuyler, *Northern Parish*, Chicago, 1960.
6. Ward, *op. cit.*, pp. 30–2.

Grammar School and Parish

The writer, as a former pupil of a Catholic grammar school, was only too well aware of the important part the school community plays in the young Catholic's life. Those who continue to the Sixth Form have little time for out of school activities of any sort; how, then, could people who had experienced this way of living for several years suddenly be integrated or re-integrated into the life of a parish? Yet this is what is expected of grammar school ex-pupils by their clergy and fellow parishioners. The writer wondered if she had overestimated the conflicting loyalties and interests held by those who have been to grammar schools, and in this investigation attempted to discover what was happening, by carefully analyzing the situation with which she was already familiar, but only personally and perhaps impressionistically.

The experiences of a number of young Catholics who had completed the course in Catholic grammar schools were therefore studied. As will subsequently appear, some were from working class homes, products of the parish school before they were selected for grammar schools; others came from middle class homes where parents were able and willing to pay for a private primary (and in some cases, secondary) education. They came, then, from vastly different social backgrounds, but they were brought together by the educational system. Does this common experience weld them into a group with shared norms and patterns of behaviour, or do they retain an allegiance to old backgrounds? If some had previously attended parochial schools, it may be asked whether such people have more in common with their former class mates from the parish, or with those with whom they received their secondary education. An attempt to find answers to such questions makes it necessary in effect to consider the extent to which the educational system operates as an agent of social change.

Thus the really basic issue of the investigation is that which was also the mainspring of Charles Booth's pioneer work on religious influences: the relationship between the values and behaviour of individuals, and the social institutions to which they belonged.[1] In the present instance, a double question was being asked, namely, do the social institutions created for educational purposes produce a different religious grouping for a minority within a section of the

---

1. Cf. T. S. Simey and M. B. Simey, *Charles Booth. Social Scientist*, Oxford, 1960: 'Booth's task was to demonstrate that a relationship, positive or negative, existed between the beliefs and behaviour of individuals, on the one hand, and the functioning of a specially selected set of social institutions, on the other.' p. 224.

community which was, by and large, socially homogeneous in the past? Or are the ties of religious loyalty sufficiently strong to enable a uniform social grouping to persist in spite of an educational system which other investigators have found was the creator of social divisions?[1]

From the writer's own experience, it looked as though the emphasis upon the importance of the school community and upon one's obligations towards it would lead to the transfer of some of the functions previously fulfilled by the parish to the grammar school. As a result, one would expect to find that young Catholics who had attended grammar schools would not tend to develop parochial loyalties, and would not take part in parish activities. It was thought, too, that those who continued to the Sixth Form, and thus very often to universities and training colleges, would develop interests which would be extra-parochial in scope, and that the brief periods spent at each stage might mean that no lasting loyalty to any formal social grouping in the Church would persist. Accordingly, they would not identify the Catholic Church with any one specific form of social grouping; for them, the beliefs and values of Catholicism would not be associated with the social structure of the parish, as they had been by earlier generations of Liverpool Catholics.

However, since there are many young Catholics in Liverpool attending grammar schools, and since this is by no means an entirely new phenomenon, it seemed unlikely that people would feel isolated. It was more probable that the majority would emerge from school with a sense of belonging to the Catholic Church; a sense, however, which they would not identify with the membership of any formal community in the Church. It seemed likely that loyalty towards the peer group would mean that the former pupils of these schools would belong to an informal grouping of Catholics. The kind of minority grouping spoken of above thus appeared to be a reality.

The hypothesis underlying these suggestions is that the Catholic grammar schools will be producing attitudes in their pupils which are different from those learned at parochial schools, and that these attitudes will lead to different behaviour. Unrelated as the grammar schools are to parochial boundaries, the pupils' interests would tend to develop in a wider setting. They would learn a different concept of the Church from that communicated through the parochial schools, and an approach to Catholicism would be encouraged which would be wider than local loyalties would permit. This would influence behaviour in relation to the social groupings of the Catholic Church.

1. E.g., Jackson and Marsden, *op. cit.*

New Cultural Developments in Catholicism

The English grammar schools, while many are newly built, also retain a great many traditions in their ethos and codes of behaviour. Because of this, and partly because of the influences mentioned above, it is only to be expected that such schools will produce a section of people vastly different from those who were educated at parochial schools. This is not primarily a question of religious values, but of cultural values and ideas. Religious beliefs may be transmitted equally well or badly by either system. But the grammar schools are intended to communicate a different set of cultural and class values from the parochial schools. Features such as leadership, independence of thought, and social responsibility all form part of their ideology. In particular, they are associated at the present time with the idea of 'getting on in the world' or social mobility.

Since such a system has been adopted by Catholics on a wider scale than previously, it seems likely, then, that not only the social structure but also the formal social organization of Roman Catholicism in Britain will be altered. One would expect that, in extending certain ideas and ways of thinking to a community which was once to a large extent socially homogeneous in Liverpool, a new cultural expression of Catholicism would develop. Just as the way in which an Italian Catholic expresses his religious beliefs in a particular *milieu* is different from the way which an Australian Catholic follows, so the rapid expansion of the Catholic middle classes in Britain will lead to changes in cultural behaviour. All will share the same basic beliefs, unaltered by differences in the environment occasioned by place or time, yet will express them differently.

But while different attitudes might develop, the process of attending Catholic schools would probably make those who have been to grammar schools conscious of belonging to a group which is religiously distinct from the wider community. This means that, in certain circumstances, the reference group of Catholicism will transcend that of social class. There will be other situations, however, when those who have attended grammar schools will perceive themselves as being different from Catholics at the lower end of the socio-economic scale (and will in turn be regarded by the latter as different); as a result, they will tend to identify with the middle class, which many of them will be entering *via* the grammar school.[1] Finally, it is suggested that the predominating reference group will be neither that of Catholicism in Liverpool as a whole, nor that of

1. E. Bott, 'The Concept of Class as a Reference Group', *Human Relations*, VII, 3 (1954), 259–85.

social class, but rather a Catholic sub-group within the wider middle class. That is, the major frame of reference will be a new cultural expression of Catholicism, one which is distinct in its attitudes and behaviour from the group to which the general body of Catholics in Liverpool have belonged in the past.

It seemed, then, that one of the consequences of an educational policy would be the disappearance of the cultural uniformity of the Catholic Church in Liverpool.[1] While changes in the social structure of Catholicism were desired and encouraged, certain other consequences for the social organization of the Church might not be greeted so enthusiastically. The new attitudes towards the Church and the members would introduce problems of adjustment in the traditional system of organization, notably in the parish. The emphasis upon the school, and the later stress upon the University Catholic Society or college organizations, would be bound to have repercussions on the parish. A clash of loyalties seemed inevitable. The role system revolving round the parish priest and grammar school parishioners, too, would have its new difficulties to encounter. Their expectations of one another's behaviour would no longer be based on a relationship of familiarity; the 'face to face' contact between priest and parishioner which made—and still makes for many—the parish a primary group, would not exist for most of those who go to grammar schools.

The research relates, therefore, to changes in the social setting of religious life which are brought about by institutional changes in another sphere. It is a study of the relationship between behaviour and values as the latter are influenced by the processes of change. Although inquiries into religious attitudes, on the one hand, and statistics of religious observance, on the other, have abounded in recent years, there is little research as yet which considers the relationship between the two. The sociologist knows remarkably little about the impact of values upon behaviour. In general sociologists tend to fight shy of discussing the relationship between values and behaviour.[2] The question of the relationship between the two is not easily avoided in the sociology of religion, however, even though analyses may be carried out with the emphasis upon individual behaviour, rather than upon values and their sociological significance.

    1. A. Spitzer, 'The Culture Organization of Catholicism', *American Catholic Sociological Review*, XIX, 1 (1958), 2–12.
    2. This timidity has been satirized by Sorokin as 'The belief that *the less a researcher of psychosocial phenomena knows about these phenomena the less partial he is, and therefore, the better his research and teaching*'. P. Sorokin, *Fads and Foibles in Modern Sociology and Related Sciences*, Chicago, 1956, p. 17. (Italics in the original.)

Education and Church Attendance

So that the place of the present research in the sociology of religion may be made clear, it seems worthwhile summarizing briefly what is known with reference to the effect of education upon religious attitudes and behaviour. In view of the vast amount of relevant literature, the main trends only are referred to, and attention is confined to studies relating to Catholicism.

One piece of information which emerges from various surveys is that in the areas investigated, as far as Catholics are concerned, the observance of religious duties improves as the standard of education rises, and that when a person has received a Catholic education, this phenomenon is even more accentuated. This has been demonstrated in different regions through censuses—and it is important to stress this: the conclusions have been reached through the analysis of statistics of actual attendance, not reported attendance. This finding has come to be regarded as a commonplace amongst investigators in the sphere of religion, although it sometimes comes as somewhat of a surprise to sociologists in other fields. An early study of this kind was carried out by Kelly in an American diocese. He had this to say:

Among the Florida Catholics the following general principle is valid: *As education increases, religious practice of the group improves* ... As a group, the best Catholics in Florida are those who have attended college while the most negligent Catholics are those who have not completed grammar school.[1]

He concludes his detailed analysis by saying: 'Education has a marked effect in fostering greater devotion to religious duties.'

In addition to the general comments, Kelly demonstrates from the diocesan statistics that the influence of attendance at a Catholic school showed itself most clearly in fidelity to devotions, such as monthly communion, which went beyond the minimum obligations of the Church.

Similar findings are reported from Lyons by Labbens and Daille.[2] These authors comment that in analyzing the patterns of church attendance, one finding is immediately apparent: the vast majority of Catholics who practise their religion have been to Catholic schools. Further analysis reveals that the most active section consists of people who have received a secondary education, including those from an intellectual *milieu*. Pin, in his notable and intensive study of a Lyons parish, also concludes that religious practice is closely cor-

1. G. Kelly, *Catholics and the Practice of the Faith*, Washington, 1946. (Italics in the original.)
2. J. Labbens and R. Daille, *La Pratique Dominicale dans l'agglomération Lyonnaise, III. L'instruction. La Ville et les Pratiquants*, Lyons, 1956.

related with education.[1] He goes on to say that the factor of education by itself is inadequate to explain variations of practice, especially when a comparison is made between the sexes; through the analysis of his material, he develops the theory that religious practice is related to a complex social phenomenon which includes factors such as occupation and education. Another report confirming that those Catholics who fulfil their religious obligations have received a higher level of education than those who do not was produced in Belgium in 1960.[2] In an analysis of religious practice according to professions, this survey carried out in the region of Namur reveals that the level of religious observance corresponds with the level of occupation, rather than to economic standing.[3]

Studies in Britain, too, have drawn attention to the apparent relationship between church attendance and social class,[4] and the statement is made in *A Survey of Social Conditions in England and Wales*, referring to the findings of recent inquiries, that 'frequent church-going becomes markedly less common with decline in the social scale.'[5] But while this seems likely to be true in the light of evidence from other countries, it has yet to be demonstrated adequately in this country. Such affirmations in British surveys must be regarded with considerable caution. For one thing, intensive studies of religious behaviour are few as yet, and comments on religion tend to be included in investigations on other topics on a level which can only be described as impressionistic. They are concerned, too, with reported behaviour rather than with the analysis of censuses of actual attendance.[6] Moreover, the distinction between the religious groups is rarely drawn with sufficient clarity. To compare the church attendance of Catholics with that of members of other religious bodies on the grounds of the degree of interest shown is a highly dubious procedure. The religious sanctions attached by the Catholic

1. E. Pin, *Pratique Religieuse et Classes Sociales dans une Paroisse Urbaine, St. Pothin à Lyon*, Paris, 1956, especially Chapter 8.

2. Centre de Recherches Socio-Religieuses, Rapport No. 59, *Etude Socio-Religieuse de l'agglomération de Namur*, Namur, 1960. Two other Belgian studies throw light on these issues, C. Leplae, *Pratique Religieuse et Milieux Sociaux*, Louvain, 1949, and J. Kerkhofs, *Godsdienstpraktijk en Sociaal Milieu*, Brussels, 1953.

3. See also, Y. Daniel, *Aspects de la Pratique Religieuse à Paris*, Paris, 1952, R. P. Luchini, *La Pratique Religieuse Dominicale dans l'agglomération Dijonnaise*, Dijon, 1959, etc.

4. Although it is not directly relevant to the present inquiry, a recent study of three of the larger sects in Britain throws interesting light upon the relationship between social class and religious behaviour, B. R. Wilson, *Sects and Society*, London, 1961.

5. A. M. Carr-Saunders, D. Caradog Jones, and C. A. Moser, Oxford, 1958, p. 261.

6. See, for instance, the study in *New Life*, XIV, 1, 2 (1958), which reports a steady decline in stated church attendance of Catholics aged fifteen to twenty-four according to the amount of Catholic education they had received.

Church to failure to attend Sunday Mass are severe, while some bodies consider weekly attendance at church as desirable rather than as a matter of obligation. Accordingly, the degree of religious vitality shown by Catholics and non-Catholics cannot validly be classed together with regard to church attendance in the way they often are.

Education and Religious Attitudes

Studies concerning the religious attitudes of educated sections of the population also abound, and students, whether at school, college or university, are particularly popular subjects for investigation. On the Continent of Europe, such inquiries can be found in a variety of countries.[1] Some are obviously more sophisticated in their methodology than others, but trends can be discerned in most of them. Many of these studies are based on replies to anonymous written questionnaires in which young people either answer open questions on religion or else express their preference for a particular category of answer.[2] The results of these investigations are often extremely interesting, especially for the insight they give into the ideas of young people living in countries which are normally termed Catholic. However, such studies tend to be descriptive rather than analytical. Although they are concerned with the effects of religious education, they do not, as a rule, go on to consider the social consequences of these attitudes.

In the United States, studies of educated sections of the public, especially students, are even more prolific. As one would expect, the methodological approaches are considerably more varied. The fact that there are so many, and that they are concerned with differently defined universes, makes it difficult to draw general conclusions from them.[3] There are a number of inquiries, however, which indicate that Catholics usually retain allegiance to their beliefs after attending colleges and universities.[4] Attention is drawn by several writers to the orthodox attitudes towards religion held by Catholic students.[5]

---

1. See, for instance, M. Fraga Iribarne and J. Tena Artigas, 'Una encuestas a los estudiantes universitarios de Madrid', *Revista Internacional de Sociología*, VIII (1950), 313–51; A. Pawelczynska, 'Les attitudes des étudiants varsoviens envers la religion', *Archives de Sociologie des Religions*, XII (1961), 107–32; P. Gouyon, 'La foi des lycéens catholiques en France', *Nouvelle Revue Théologique*, LXXII, 10 (1950), 1028–49.
2. As, for instance, in P. N. De Volder, 'Inquiry into the Religious Life of Catholic Intellectuals', *Journal of Social Psychology*, XXVIII, 1 (1948), 39–56.
3. There is an excellent summary, heavily documented, of studies of the religion of American students by H. Carrier, 'La Religion des Etudiants Américains', *Archives de Sociologie des Religions*, XII (1961), 89–106.
4. See E. H. Nowlan, 'The Picture of the "Catholic" which emerges from Attitude Tests', *Lumen Vitae*, XII, 2 (1957), 274–85.
5. For example, A. R. Gilliland, 'Changes in Religious Beliefs of College Students', *Journal of Social Psychology*, XXXVII, 1 (1953), 113–16.

However, like European investigations, these studies are psychological, and generally speaking are not concerned with the relationship between values and institutional behaviour.

So there are studies, on the one hand, of observed behaviour, and, on the other, of attitudes towards religion. Probably the only major piece of work concerned with the effect of education upon religious behaviour in an institutional context is Fichter's study of a parochial school in the United States.[1] Apart from investigations describing the ways in which immigrants adapt to a new culture,[2] little research has been carried out so far to show how changes are brought about in religious institutions through educational change.[3] There seems, therefore, to be every justification for beginning to investigate the relationships between education and religious behaviour and attitudes, with a view to understanding the consequences which educational changes have for religious institutions and groups. It is unfortunate that in the enthusiasm for objective information, the study of behaviour has been divorced from the study of attitudes in the sociology of religion.[4] It seems evident that the two cannot be considered separately in this way, and the present inquiry attempts to study social behaviour in the light of attitudes. It is hoped, too, that both may be seen in the background of their social setting, so that their sociological implications may appear more clearly. In this way, it may be possible to observe and describe some of the dynamic factors involved in change while they are actually taking place.

The Present Inquiry

In short, the investigation was designed to find out the relationships which a section of the former pupils of Catholic grammar schools in Liverpool had with the formal groupings of the Church. At the same time, it was hoped to discover how they saw themselves and other Catholics in relation to these groupings. This work was carried out through intensive interviewing. The views of parish priests, teachers and parishioners were then examined, again through interviews, to discover how others who were involved in the same situation perceived and evaluated it and the relationships within it. Finally,

1. Op. cit.
2. Such as W. Lloyd Warner and L. Srole, The Social Systems of American Ethnic Groups, New Haven, 1945.
3. A notable contribution to the understanding of religious groups in a contemporary social context is G. E. Lenski, The Religious Factor, New York, 1961.
4. Since this study was begun, a notable exception to this trend has appeared, H. Carrier, Psycho-Sociologie de l'appartenance religieuse, Rome, 1960. The reception given to this work makes it plain that many currently engaged in socio-religious research welcome a more profound approach to the study of religious phenomena.

another piece of fieldwork was carried out in a parish to test the validity of certain hypotheses which had emerged in the course of the inquiry.

In the pages which follow, the methodology and its implications are described first of all. The data obtained from the interviews are then analyzed in two ways; firstly, in terms of social background, and secondly in terms of the expression of religious views. The investigation then goes on to consider how far these views were influenced by the school, for it is on this hypothesis that much of what follows depends. Next, the image of the parish in the eyes of the former pupils of Catholic grammar schools was studied, rather than the parochial system as a whole, for it is only when the attitudes of pupils are described that their behaviour in relation to this system becomes intelligible. Since one might expect that these Catholics would develop loyalties to Catholic organizations that transcend parochial boundaries, attention is then turned to extra-parochial associations. Particular consideration is given in the analysis to the University Catholic Society, for its existence is a recognition of the fact that social change produces new religious needs which must be met institutionally. In these ways, all the formal groupings of Catholicism in Liverpool are considered. But informal groupings are a factor which must also be given special consideration; this is why leisure time activities and patterns of friendship are described. This section is not an afterthought, but an integral part of the research, revealing not only the extent to which these young people are in contact with other Catholics of a similar background, but also the closeness of their relationships with the wider community.

Finally, there is a brief parochial study in which the impact of educational change is considered from another angle. This was designed to do two things; firstly, to determine the proportion of active parishioners who had attended grammar schools, and secondly, to discover how active parishioners perceived and evaluated the attitudes and behaviour of Catholics who had been to grammar schools.

This study is essentially an exploratory one, and it was necessarily restricted in scope. Bearing this in mind, it seemed more worthwhile to describe a small section of people in detail rather than to consider a wider population and be forced to restrict the analysis to subjects which would have been merely superficial. As a result, the conclusions are tentative, and some of them may be open to criticism. But the function of investigations such as this is not to produce final conclusions (if these can ever be made), but rather to probe promising areas, to discover which are blind alleys, and which are those which will lead to a firmer understanding of social realities. The sociology of religion abounds with publications which purport to offer unassailable findings. But the amount now available of an imaginative kind, which illuminates the relationship between religious values, behaviour and social institutions, is lamentably small. It seems that a few explorations in the dark will eventually serve the subject better than another plodding step whose conclusions are irrefutable, even though they may quickly be shown to be inadequate. Indeed, the sooner they are surpassed, the more quickly the study will advance. It is hoped that through this analysis of behaviour and attitudes, and especially through the emphasis upon the ways in which people themselves perceive the truth about themselves, some useful light may be thrown upon what happens to traditional values and institutions within a society when a part of the wider social system is deliberately altered.

In the interests of social welfare, legislators and administrators accept a responsibility to formulate and apply new social policies; their courage needs to be matched equally responsibly by the sociologist, whose task it should be to discover the results of administrative action, and why it is that what is done has so often unintended consequences.

Chapter 2

THE INVESTIGATION AND ITS
METHODOLOGICAL IMPLICATIONS

It has already been explained that the aim of this present research was to produce results which would throw light on the more serious problems of the religious life in the age in which we live. It was decided, therefore, to interview a small number of people intensively, rather than to deal with a larger group and thus have to restrict the amount and significance of the evidence which could be collected. Since the investigator was interested in what happens to Catholics who become socially mobile, those who had completed the grammar school course seemed best suited to the purpose. After preliminary interviews had been carried out, the scope of this study was eventually determined. It consisted of all Catholics leaving Catholic grammar schools in the City of Liverpool in a selected year, after having spent two or more years in the Sixth Form, whose address at the time of leaving was in the city, and who were still resident within the city boundaries at the time of the fieldwork.[1] Those studying away from Liverpool for part of the year were included because they had not left home.

As the primary interest of the investigation was in the influences of the grammar school on adolescent behaviour and attitudes, the study was confined to this group. Although those who remain to the Sixth Form are in the minority at the moment, there is a growing stress upon the importance of the last years, and the schools themselves have always encouraged pupils to stay on. It is also certain that increasing numbers will complete the Sixth Form course in the future. Moreover, the Sixth Form is generally the necessary preliminary for admission to universities and colleges, and this thereby covered the section of the population most likely to move into the higher professions. Only those who stayed in the Sixth Form for two or more years were included; this decision was due partly to convenience, but also because the evidence produced by the head-teachers indicated that those who left after only one year in the Sixth Form had more in common with those who left to take jobs

1. There were three exceptions to this: two people were living in the city's housing estates outside the boundary line, and another person was living temporarily with relatives, again outside the boundary, but the parents' address was within the city limits.

before the end of the course, than with those who completed two
years or more in the Sixth Form.

The study was confined to the City of Liverpool for practical
reasons. Most of the schools drew a proportion of their pupils from
places further afield, within a radius of thirty miles, including
Widnes and Warrington, and, on the other side of the River Mersey,
from the Wirral. The interviewer could not hope to cover such a
widely scattered group. Moreover, by restricting the area, information about the parishes in which those who were interviewed lived
could be obtained without too much difficulty. It would have been
interesting to have included those who live away from home, but
they form a separate section. In any case, it would have been
impossible to interview the latter personally, and the problems
involved in postal questionnaires, notably the high failure rate,
made it advisable to limit the research in this way.

After some deliberation, it was decided to study those who had left
school three years before the time the fieldwork was carried out.[1]
They had had time to evaluate their school experiences and to be on
the way to settling in their occupations. A study of an older group
might have been more valuable in some respects, but it was sufficiently difficult to locate those who had left comparatively recently.

There are at present ten Catholic grammar schools in the City of
Liverpool. One of the boys' schools was built only recently and had
no Sixth Form leavers at the date chosen. The universe, then, consisted of ex-pupils of three boys' and six girls' schools. Lists were obtained of all those Catholics who left in the year selected, after two
or more years in the Sixth Form. Those who did not live in the city
were excluded immediately, and one hundred and eleven names were
left. Of these, however, twenty had to be eliminated because two sets
of lists were defective. Some of those eliminated (after a considerable
amount of time had been wasted tracing them) had left home, several
had spent only one year in the Sixth Form, and a couple on the list
were not Catholics. The final universe of study, then, totalled ninety-
one. Eighty-four interviews were completed, and by coincidence
there were forty-two of each sex. There was a failure rate of 7·7 per
cent. No one refused to be interviewed, but a couple broke appointments, and it proved impossible to get in touch with the others.
Table 1 shows the number of respondents from each school.

1. In view of the extraordinary amount of speculation amongst Catholics in
Liverpool, following the publication of Dr. Ward's *Priests and People*, as to the
identity of 'St. Catherine's parish', it seems worthwhile to emphasize strongly
that during the initial stages of the fieldwork many interviews were carried out
with the former pupils of a variety of years. Except in the very early stages, respondents were not told which interviews would be used in the ultimate analysis. It
would be unwise, therefore, for anyone to attempt to identify either the year or
an individual.

TABLE 1

Number of Respondents from Nine Catholic Grammar Schools

	Male	Female	Total
Boys' Schools: 1	15	0	15
2	15	0	15
3	12	0	12
Girls' Schools: 4	0	11	11
5	0	14	14
6	0	1	1
7	0	8	8
8	0	7	7
9	0	1	1
Total	42	42	84

The Inquiry

A structured interview was used to obtain information from this group; the interview schedule can be found in Appendix I. All the interviews were carried out by the writer. The length of the interviews varied from slightly under half an hour to over two hours; people not only varied in their loquacity, but also several sections of the schedule applied only to some of those who were interviewed.

It proved extremely difficult to locate many of the respondents. For a start, the addresses were spread throughout the city, and finding them involved a good deal of time and travelling. The time of the fieldwork, May to October, meant that university students were doing final examinations at the beginning of the period; holidays, too, made contacts difficult. Most of the students were working during the vacation. One student, for instance, was interviewed before going on night work, and the interview had to be split and carried out on two consecutive days. There was also the problem that the lists of addresses were at least three years old. More than 20 per cent of the universe had moved from the addresses given by the schools. (In fact, one or two had moved before leaving school.) The new addresses were discovered in a variety of ways; from the telephone directory (not so obvious a source as it might seem, since the people being sought were not themselves the subscribers, and sometimes had names of which a long list appeared in the directory), from the files of the University Catholic Society, and from friends. Occasionally, too,

TABLE 2

Interview Arrangements

Call, interview	3
Saw, made appointment	12
Call, made appt.	14
Letter, appt.	8
Phone, appt.	7
Call, family seen, recall, appt.	8
Phone, appt, half interview, appt. broken, phone, appt.	1
Call, family made appt., recall, respondent out, letter, second letter, appt.	1
Call, saw family, recall, interview postponed, letter, appt.	1
Call, saw family, phone, appt.	1
Call, no reply, recall, saw family, letter, appt...	3
Call, no reply, recall, saw family, recall, appt.	2
Call, no reply, recall, saw family, phone, appt.	2
Call, no reply, letter, appt.	2
Call, no reply, recall, saw family, appt.	2
Call, no reply, phone, appt.	2
Call, no reply, recall, no reply, recall, saw family, appt.	1
Call, away, letter, recall, no reply, recall, appt.	1
Call, away, letter, recall, saw family, appt.	1
Letter, phone, appt.	1
Letter, two phone calls, appt.	1
Letter, appt., call, no reply, letter, appt.	1
Call, saw family, two letters, appt.	1
Call, moved, call at new address, saw family, letter, appt.	1
Call, appt., letter refusing, letter, appt...	1
Call, no reply, saw, appt.	1
Three calls, no reply, letter, appt.	1
Two calls, no reply, phone, away, phone, appt.	1
Saw, appt., twice broken, letter, phone	1
Moved, letter, moved, letter forwarded, appt.	1
Call, away, recall, saw family, phone, appt.	1
Total	84

letters were forwarded from old addresses. Table 2 should make it clear that the difficulties of contacting people have not been exaggerated.

When the first approach requesting an interview was made, nearly all were extremely co-operative, and even enthusiastic. One young man, for instance, greeted the visitor by exclaiming, 'Gosh, yes!' and promised that if the interviewer would return in a day or two he would 'tidy all this', indicating his family and the pleasant room in which they were sitting. The fact that the majority enjoyed the interview was clear from their willingness to allow it to become protracted, and from the way in which the interviewer was frequently asked to stay longer to talk about the survey. It seems more than likely that several welcomed the interview as an opportunity to express views—this was a matter of personal concern. As one of them wrote, 'As I imagine will be the case with the other characters on your list, it is no bother for me to answer any questions about myself, but rather a great pleasure, being as great an egotist as the next man.' Few made any difficulties about being interviewed.

Many questions were asked about the survey, and the interviewer's own plans. Often people said they envied her for having such an easy job, a view which the investigator occasionally found hard to share, especially on the many days when several fruitless visits had been paid, during a summer which seemed to have more than its share of rainfall. In general, the questions were taken very seriously; one or two of the respondents treated them all rather like an examination, giving them the most conscientious attention. Sometimes a person felt he could not give an answer on the spur of the moment and asked to be allowed to return to the point later.

Place of Interview

Most of the interviews took place in the respondents' own homes. This had various advantages, in that it meant that they were at their ease, and it was possible to supplement the information given in the interviews by general observation. But it had its disadvantages, too. For example, although it was stressed that the interview was confidential, in a handful of them someone else was present for part of the time, and it was impossible to ask them to leave without being rude. Sometimes, too, mothers brought in tea or coffee, and in these cases the interview was brought to a temporary halt. Another disadvantage in some homes was noise, and more than once the interviewer had to compete with television programmes in the adjoining room.

There were few interviews in respondents' own homes where the interviewer was not treated as a guest. Often when appointments had been made, the interviewer was introduced to all the members of the family, normally by her Christian name; occasionally she was asked if she minded being called by her first name, but most did this as a matter of course. Many immediately 'placed' the interviewer as a member of the 'in-group', in terms of her school, family, and sometimes even friends; others took time to do this, but it is important to note that a good many thought it necessary to do so before the interview could begin. Even parents took part on occasion, especially when they themselves had been to Catholic grammar schools in the city or had taken part in the activities organized by people who had. One mother, for instance, took several minutes 'placing' the interviewer, then left with a smile, saying, 'I'm happy now I've "placed" you!' This factor seemed to be the most important for many people in accepting the interviewer. Once she had been identified as a member of the in-group, a social relationship was established which was satisfactory to the respondents.[1]

The extent to which explanations of the survey were given to members of the family when calls were fruitless varied according to the circumstances. Clearly, the visit of the interviewer caused speculation in some homes, and this had its uses; curiosity made people stay at home at the time the mysterious visitor was expected back. Others found an explanation for themselves, like the little girl who listened to the interviewer's careful explanation to her mother; she, with an *entourage* of small friends, escorted the interviewer down the flights of stairs from the flat where they lived, confiding, 'I thought you was our Tony's girlfriend.'

It was apparent even in the early stages, however, that all the interviews could not be carried out in respondents' own homes. In some houses no room was available. As one young man who was willing to be interviewed pointed out, 'The question is, where? You see, at home, I'm afraid there aren't the amenities for such an interview, unless you like to compete with television.' Before any of the interviews were carried out, one of the headteachers predicted that some would be reluctant to be interviewed in their own homes: 'They'll make it clear to you that this may be where they came from, but that it's not where they're stopping.' It was evident that whatever motives people might have for being unwilling to be interviewed in their own homes, it was essential to offer an alternative meeting place at the first approach. It was mentioned, therefore, that the interview could take place either in the home or in the Department of Social Science. About a quarter chose the latter. Some were students at Liverpool University and suggested the Department would be mutually convenient, especially if they lived a good way out of the city centre.

It proved more difficult, as one would expect, to establish a relaxed atmosphere in an empty lecture room, especially as the room overlooked a building site. As a result, several interviews were punctuated with the noise of drilling. Even with the use of the

1. Cf. the results of the investigations carried out by G. E. Lenski and J. C. Leggett, 'Caste, Class and Deference in the Research Interview', *American Journal of Sociology*, LXV, 5 (1960), especially pp. 463 and 467.

Department, not everyone was catered for, since the room was not available in the evenings. The Students' Union was used for several interviews; the library, the coffee bar, the Common Lounge, were all tried, and each proved more difficult than the last. But somehow or other, eighty-four interviews were completed, and the enthusiasm and interest of those who were interviewed made the fieldwork an exciting and enjoyable experience which more than compensated for the tedium of repeated calls.

Additional Fieldwork

A number of interviews were also carried out with former pupils of the nine schools from different years. These have not been used in the final analysis, but were valuable in giving insight into the situation as a whole. In the preliminary stages of the inquiry, the heads of the nine schools were approached and an interview requested. Eight were interviewed, and they were extremely helpful in giving general comments. Two of the headteachers were kind enough to supply additional information and help throughout the investigation. Lists were obtained from all the schools, and one headteacher even went so far as to allow the interviewer access to the school files.

After the survey of the former pupils of the grammar schools had been completed, additional fieldwork was carried out to discover the views of the parish priests. Sixteen parish priests were interviewed and were very helpful. Others were encountered in the course of the study, but it must be stressed that the only information used in Chapters 6 and 7 was obtained from priests who stated their views in some detail and were willing to co-operate more generally. Priests concerned with extra-parochial organizations, including five university chaplains and the chaplains of some of the extra-parochial organizations in Liverpool, were also interviewed.

A considerable amount of time was spent visiting various organizations which were designed to cater for the needs and interests of the former pupils of Catholic grammar schools; their officers were often interviewed. This section of the fieldwork covered a wide range of activities, from attending services to going to dances, from being taken on tours of public houses frequented by the former pupils of the boys' schools, to helping run a club for youngsters. Throughout the three years spent on this research, numerous lectures, meetings, and conferences relevant to the questions discussed in it were attended, including a course designed to prepare those who had been educated in Catholic grammar schools to train as youth leaders. Extensive use was also made of documentary sources, especially programmes, handbooks and reports of the different organizations.

A separate piece of fieldwork was undertaken in a parish; this was designed to test the validity of certain hypotheses which had emerged from the findings of the main survey. Details of this inquiry and the results are described in Chapter 11.

The Implications of the Fieldwork

It should be explained that the research was not conducted only by way of analyzing the information collected in the manner which has been described. Although the inquiry was planned in some detail in order to provide a means of testing certain hypotheses which had been previously formulated, the direction of the research was much influenced by the experiences of the fieldwork itself.

At the outset, convinced that impartiality was the most desirable objective in the interview and that the intrusion of the personality of the investigator must be reduced to a minimum, an attempt was made to carry out fieldwork specifically directed to the obtaining of so-called 'objective' information, which admitted only one interpretation. This motive came from two sources; firstly and chiefly, from the work of sociologists who emphasize the importance of basing social investigation upon 'scientific' foundations, and the need to reduce the instruments of research to uniformity. Secondly, and by implication rather than by precept, this resulted from the current trend in socio-religious research on the Continent of Europe, which is based largely upon statistical analysis, and draws attention to the importance of objective indications of religious vitality, such as censuses of church attendance and baptismal figures. Information was obtained in this way concerning, for instance, membership of religious organizations, which was easily analyzed and apparently objective; but it must also be recorded that it proved to be largely useless in understanding the processes of social change.

Confronted with this failure, and being by this time more aware of the limitations of contemporary research in the sociology of religion precisely because it has largely confined itself to data which can be analyzed statistically, a somewhat more cautious and sophisticated approach proved necessary. Proceeding with more thought and less reliance on the dogmatic assertions of a few sociologists, the writer carried out the study described in this book in the belief that the investigator obtains an understanding of a social situation only in so far as he is prepared to accept the fact that he is a part of the human relationships he is investigating. The concept of objectivity in social research derives from analogy, no longer tenable, with the natural sciences. The assumption that what is measured and studied is left unchanged by the study itself was rapidly found to be invalid, despite the fact that the social scientist has been urged so frequently to imitate the natural sciences in this regard. The investigator's involvement in the social processes he is investigating has been deprecated, but in the opinion of the writer, to deny the involvement of the investigator is to reject reality. To ignore involvement is, indeed, to waste an opportunity to develop understanding. In sum, the writer maintains that the social investigator succeeds in obtaining an understanding of a social situation only to the extent to which he is prepared to accept himself as being the initiator of a social relationship, and to use that relationship to the best of his ability as a means of understanding behaviour in its social context.

It is worthwhile noting that this position which has been largely neglected in social research in the sphere of religion was accepted by one of the pioneers of the empirical approach to religious groups, Charles Booth:

Yet though intellectually he strove to remain detached, he was at the same time happy to confess that he enjoyed participating in the life he observed, and was always willing to accept the fact that his mere presence amidst any group necessarily involved him in a relationship with its members.[1]

Membership of the In-Group

It was, indeed, impossible in any event for the interviewer to remain at a distance from the subject matter of her researches. Furthermore, as a Catholic who had been educated at one of the schools included in the survey, she was already involved in the social situation being studied. In the initial stages, this involvement was a source of embarrassment, in that people sometimes placed her in the in-group, and reacted accordingly, for the ways in which she was welcomed and her visits treated as social occasions caused concern sometimes at this apparent disregard of her professional role. Fortunately, it soon became evident that being a member of the in-group, far from being a hindrance, was without doubt the greatest advantage the investigator had. The preliminary interviews made it plain that those who placed the interviewer as a member of the in-group were much more ready to talk freely, and especially to express criticisms, than those who were not aware of the fact.[2] The importance of membership of the in-group should become apparent in the chapters which follow. Chapter 4, especially, reveals how strongly many of those who were interviewed were conscious of being members of a minority group, and how defensive their attitudes sometimes were towards those who did not share their views.

1. Simey, *op. cit.*, p. 143. See also the similar approach taken by W. Lloyd Warner and P. S. Lunt, *The Social Life of a Modern Community*, New Haven, 1941, p. 48.

2. It is interesting to see in this context how many writers engaged in research into religious movements have adopted amongst their techniques that of participant observation and have lived temporarily as members of the groups studied.

Similar findings are reported by Ward, who compared attitudes towards a 'detached observer' and a known Catholic, with those towards himself, a priest immediately visible as such. It was found that the priest achieved acceptance more easily, but that there were no significant differences between the interviews carried out by the priest and the interviewer known as a Catholic. The interviewer whose religious affiliation was not known 'appeared to encounter a desire "not to let the side down", which resulted in an almost complete absence of critical comment or information which might have appeared unfavourable to the Church.'[1]

These conclusions, therefore, led to the decision that the interviewer should introduce herself in the role of someone carrying out research, and that she should mention in the request for an interview that she, like those she was approaching, was a former pupil of a Catholic grammar school in Liverpool. This was to be done by way of explaining her interest in the subject, for the interviewer was often asked how she had come to select the topic for research. This made it clear that an explanation was usually necessary, though it was not always required. A considerable number placed the interviewer immediately as a member of the in-group and welcomed her as such. The decision that the introduction should take this form, rather than that the interviewer should describe herself as a Catholic, was made on the ground that those who had attended Catholic grammar schools and were still Catholics would probably infer that the interviewer was also a Catholic and would therefore respond freely; those who were no longer Catholics, on the other hand, would not assume anything of the kind. This was based upon the observation that people being interviewed come to believe that the interviewer shares their views, irrespective of the actual fact. A striking example of this was the reaction of a woman interviewed by the writer in the course of a survey carried out by another investigator in an Anglican parish, who appealed to the interviewer, saying, 'Don't you think we Protestants should stick together like the Jews and the Catholics do?'

It was realized that an introduction of this kind might prejudice

1. C. K. Ward, 'Some Aspects of the Social Structure of a Roman Catholic Parish', *The Sociological Review*, N.S., VI, 1, (1958), p. 77. See also, the findings of A. Spitzer, 'Aspects of Religious Life in Tepoztlàn', *Anthropological Quarterly*, XXX, 1 (1957), 1–17; and Father Victor, *Chathiath. A Parish of Kerala*, Kottayam, 1961, where attempts made by the author to collect data on religion proved largely a failure because the interviewers had no understanding of the respondents' religious views. Subsequent research carried out by the present writer further confirmed this; in interviewing members of a university religious group in another city, without her own views being revealed, it was found that the members were anxous that a favourable impression should be given to the interviewer. A member who was on the point of revealing some of the group's problems was quickly suppressed by the others.

those who no longer regarded themselves as Catholics, in that they might be hostile, or reluctant to discuss their religious views. But it was hoped that the advantages would justify taking the chance, and the results amply confirmed that this was so. Many were very critical throughout the interview of social groupings within the Catholic Church; it was often assumed that the interviewer would share their criticisms, and comments such as, 'You know what it's like', or 'You know what I mean', were frequent.

It must also be pointed out that the issue as to which role the interviewer should play was not one which could be evaded, for she was often immediately asked if she was a Catholic. One young man who no longer regarded himself as one asked this question before any form of introduction had been made, beyond a letter briefly outlining the survey and requesting an interview. Another person with similar views stopped her in the middle of the interview to inquire, 'Are you a Catholic? A *practising* Catholic?' On receiving the answer, he continued, 'I thought so. It's only Catholics who are interested in things like that.'[1] The interview then continued, his remarks being as critical after the question as before. A girl, again, who had been very critical about the religious lessons in the Sixth Form, suddenly asked the same question. On receiving the answer, she showed great relief that she had not in fact expressed these views to someone outside the in-group.

A very valuable aid in the fieldwork was that the interviewer was familiar with the jargon used within the group, and this eliminated the need for explanations which might have bored respondents and caused the interviews to flag. The importance of this point will be appreciated by those who are aware of the tremendous extent to which Catholics use terms amongst themselves which are not familiar to those outside the group.[2] It must be remembered that those who were interviewed came from homes where at least one parent was a Catholic, that all had attended Catholic secondary schools, and that nearly all had attended a Catholic primary school. The majority had close Catholic friends, and a high proportion had attended Catholic training colleges. It can be understood, then, how accustomed such a group were in talking about religion or religious groups to expressing themselves in terms peculiar to the sub-culture in which they had grown up.

1. This can be compared with the surprise shown by a girl at the answer to a similar question, 'because it's usually only non-Catholics who are interested in that sort of thing.'

2. Many words which are used frequently by Catholics have a different usage in ordinary speech in Britain, e.g. 'assumption', 'mass', 'office', 'host', etc., quite apart from complex doctrinal references which are meaningless to those who are not familiar with them.

In the interviews with the priests, too, the fact that the interviewer was a Catholic was usually particularly helpful. In the few interviews where this seemed unimportant, the information given was not detailed. In general, they were much more concerned to establish the interviewer's *bona fides* as a Catholic than as a sociologist. More than one stated flatly that he would not be prepared to state his views so frankly to a non-Catholic. As one priest put it before starting the interview, 'Are you a Catholic? Good, now I can talk freely.' The parish priests were aware that the information which they supplied would be used in the research, unless, as sometimes happened, certain items were expressly excluded from this permission. The clue to the reluctance of some to give information to non-Catholics appears to lie in the references some made to a recent publication which they considered treated Catholicism and superstition as synonymous. Their distrust, then, was not directed at the collecting of information, for they were most co-operative, but at the use to which the results might be put. An additional advantage in the course of the interviews with the clergy was that several informally recommended the interviewer to others, and this was invaluable, especially in gaining access to meetings and documentary sources.

One of the major advantages of being a member of the in-group was that the interviewer was able to join in activities without awkward preliminaries, often going to a club meeting or a dance, for example, with a member who shared a similar educational background. When meeting the officers, too, it was easy to establish contact. It was accepted without question that another Catholic should be interested in Catholic organizations, and answers were readily given. Like the priests, they introduced the interviewer to others who could give information. The practical and ethical problems of participant observation were avoided because the interviewer was already a member of the group.[1] Most important of all, perhaps, the carrying out of this investigation did not involve a departure from group norms. Many of those who were interviewed were students and therefore appreciated the interviewer's position; their sympathy in this matter was undoubtedly one of the reasons for their co-operative attitude. There were, therefore, no problems about the interviewer being 'discovered'. In the circumstances, this was particularly valuable since the close contact which existed between the former pupils of Catholic grammar schools meant that news about the inquiry was transmitted

---

1. For discussion of problems encountered in using this technique, see E. Mumford, 'Participant Observation in Industry: An Evaluation', *Occupational Psychology*, XXXII, 3 (1958), 153–61; W. F. Whyte, *Street Corner Society*, Chicago, 1943; and R. Poblete, 'Sociological Approach to the Sects', *Social Compass*, VII, 5, 383–406.

both speedily and widely; in any event, attempts to conceal the investigation would probably have been abortive.[1]

Taking the view, then, that the investigator as a member of the in-group was in a particularly advantageous position to obtain information, the whole emphasis in the study was placed upon the ways in which those who were involved in the situation which was being investigated, priests, the former pupils of grammar schools, their teachers, and active parishioners, formed their opinions about it. Realizing the sterility of techniques which produce objective information and yet contribute little to the deeper understanding of the processes involved in social change, the implications of W. I. Thomas's dictum were accepted to the full: 'If men define situations as real, they are real in their consequences.'[2] The findings of C. K. Ward's study of a Liverpool parish make it plain that advances will be made in the understanding of socio-religious phenomena only by taking into account the ways in which those who participate in a religious system perceive and evaluate that system. A conspicuous illustration of why this should be done can be seen amongst the results of the present study in the number of occasions where pluralistic ignorance was found to exist; by considering the different ways people perceived what was happening, it could be seen how confusions about role behaviour, for instance, had arisen.[3]

Up to the present time, too much attention has been directed in the sociology of religion to the observation of the behaviour of religious groups in the narrow sense; it has been forgotten that it is the attitudes and values of the members that make the system what it is. The behaviour and attitudes of a group cannot be divorced, even for the purposes of analysis. No real understanding can be obtained without considering not only the situation as the investigator observes it, but also the ways in which the participants perceive it to exist. Accordingly, to understand, instead of only to describe, the ways in which young Catholics behaved in relation to the traditional institution of the parish, for instance, the focus of the inquiry was not the parish itself, but the reactions of its members. As a result, much of the information collected in this survey cannot be put into tables. Yet it is the contention of the writer that a deeper knowledge of the working of social systems can be achieved in this way, that is, by analysis of

1. Those who were interviewed were told that many people like themselves would be interviewed and the results would be prejudiced if the exact questions were known. Respondents were extraordinarily co-operative in their discretion in this respect.
2. *The Child in America*, (with Dorothy Swaine Thomas), New York, 1928, 1929, 1932, p. 22, cited by E. H. Volkart, *Social Behavior and Personality. Contributions of W. I. Thomas to Theory and Social Research*, New York, 1951, p. 14.
3. This position is developed by the writer in 'Perception in Socio-Religious Research', *Sociologia Religiosa*, VII, 9–10 (1963), 65–70.

situations rather than counting heads. Some of the most fruitful information came in the course of answers which defy tabulation. The results make it clear that the value of the interview in socio-religious research cannot be overestimated; the ways in which those who were interviewed approached questions and their reaction to the interviewer produced very interesting material.

To complement this approach, an attempt was made to carry out a study in a parish of membership of parochial organizations according to educational background. This, it was hoped, would produce more information which would permit only one interpretation, to support the rest of the fieldwork. This did in fact produce useful evidence; but even some of that was found to be based on the impressions of those who were interviewed, in exactly the same way as the major part of the fieldwork. The investigator was often dependent on the memories of officers of organizations, which obviously varied in reliability. Sooner or later, it was clear that any pretence to 'objectivity' in such a piece of fieldwork would have to be abandoned. What if a person's name was on a register but he rarely attended meetings? Could one equate, say, a member of the St. Vincent de Paul Society who attended a meeting and carried out a substantial work duty each week with someone who occasionally had a drink in the Men's Club? Decisions involving the personal element had to be made at every point.

Further Implications of the Fieldwork

Other issues arising from the fieldwork are relevant not only to the sociology of religion, but to social investigation in general. Some of the problems were universal and inevitable. For instance, people were being asked to remember activities over a period of years and to recall memories which were often vague. But it must be stressed that the interviewer's interest was in their opinions and evaluations at the time of the fieldwork. No pretence is made that their comments, on school activities, for example, reflected their feelings at the time they were at school; what was wanted was information on how they saw matters later.

The fact that the group being studied had received a high level of education produced its own problems. The linguistic sophistication of those who were interviewed made it difficult to ask questions which were uniformly meaningful. Some questions were, of course, left deliberately vague to see what reactions they would provoke. But apparently simple questions were often interpreted very differently. It is clear that this is a factor to be faced in interviewing an educated group. Another feature of this problem was the careful consideration given to the questions; answers often began, 'It all depends . . .'

People were unwilling to make flat statements without reservations and wanted to weigh up evidence, which naturally made analysis a very frustrating process. This is not simply a part of the limitations of a particular piece of fieldwork but rather a problem for social methodology which can only be tackled by introducing more sensitive techniques into research. A great deal of the social research carried out in this country has been confined to a working-class population, where it is apparently easier to get direct statements which can be compared. Does this make the information obtained any more valid? This is, to say the least of it, open to question.

Another characteristic feature of the replies was the use of colloquialisms, and mannerisms, such as 'definitely', 'personally', and 'actually'. Those interviewed also tended to express their views in an extreme form. No attempt has been made, therefore, to tabulate opinions on scales according to the degree of enthusiasm. Some endeavour has been made to discriminate in the chapters which follow, but the writer is unwilling to place answers in categories which are anything more than obvious. When reservations are made in the text, it is clear what is being done, and the reader can evaluate the validity of this for himself; when they are made in tables, it is less obvious, and may be misleading in the extreme. To communicate the feeling of the replies, extensive use has been made of extracts from interviews. The elaborate ways in which these people respond have the advantage of showing that the answer, 'I don't know' was generally a firm statement of inability to reply, not mere boredom or lack of comprehension.

Many of the questions in the interview appear to overlap, as in fact they do. But this was a deliberate policy, an attempt to capture every possible activity. Experience showed that this caution was justified, and memories were often evoked by apparently superfluous questions. The resulting length of the interview was a strain on both the respondents and the investigator, but the writer is convinced by the results that this reduced inconsistencies.

The results of the fieldwork, then, often defy statistical analysis. To produce a clear description of a uniform trend would be emotionally satisfying—but not intellectually so. Like those who were interviewed, the writer has had to make reservations in outlining even the most obvious trends. The investigation has left her convinced of the outstanding need in the sociology of religion to develop techniques of research which are sensitive to the more subtle ways in which values affect behaviour.

Chapter 3

THE SOCIAL BACKGROUND OF THE FORMER PUPILS OF CATHOLIC GRAMMAR SCHOOLS

SOME of the changes which are taking place in the social structure and systems of Roman Catholicism in Liverpool are immediately visible. There is a great contrast, for instance, between the older churches in and around the central areas and the newer ones to be found on recently developed housing estates. In the older districts, it is not unusual for a walk of less than half an hour to lead to four or even more Catholic churches. In the midst of the densely populated areas, such churches, few of them distinguished architecturally, attract great loyalty from their parishioners, a sentiment almost akin to patriotism. With their dark interiors, their sanctuary lamps and statues cast in similar moulds, these churches are strikingly alike. They never seem to be empty, and the comings and goings are much the same from one to another. Growing up in such a context, the young Catholic becomes accustomed to the regular features: to the old man or woman who always seems to be there; the small children running in and out to pay a speedy visit, one scarcely bigger than the rest admonishing them to make decorous genuflections; the murmur as an old person prays aloud; the clatter of the rosary beads as they fall through the fingers on to the wooden bench.

It is this aspect of Roman Catholicism in Liverpool which is best known to the outsider. It is this, together with the traditional devotion to the patriarchal parish priest, which forms the standby of the journalist. The old hostility between Catholic and Protestant in the city is frequently cited; the words, 'God bless our Canon', inscribed on a wall by Catholics in one area, have their counterpart in the dedication on a wall in the north end of the city, 'King Billy is a hero'. But like most popular conceptions, this familiar aspect of Liverpool Catholicism is somewhat out-of-date.

There is another side to Catholicism in the city which is developing rapidly, so rapidly that its consequences have not yet made themselves fully felt. The churches on the new housing estates are in sharp contrast to the older buildings. Simpler in design and often better adapted to the liturgy or public worship of the Catholic Church, their light and uncluttered interiors with modern and angular representations of Christ and the saints cannot but strike one as being harshly different from the older churches. Instead of being squashed between the houses and reduced like them to a uniform grime, the new churches often stand on plots of land as yet uncultivated. Yet even here, there is the concession to popular feeling, and a large statue of the Sacred Heart or Our Lady of Lourdes makes this setting a little more familiar. The Catholic population of the City Corporation's new housing estates is extremely high, and looking at such churches, one wonders how these changes in surroundings will affect the religious lives, on the one hand of people accustomed to a very different setting, and, on the other, of growing children. Like the new homes, the churches reflect a different way of living from the old familiar background.

And in between the two extremes, there are the churches in the suburbs, some more modern in design than others, yet most remarkably similar to those in the central districts; statues or murals which do not fit into the traditional mould do not tend to be viewed with approval. It is as if social mobility for these people did not demand a reaction, but only the familiar in a better setting. On Sundays, the growing numbers of cars outside such churches demonstrate the changes in social structure which are taking place.

Within the churches, too, the old traditions exist side by side with changing ideas. The somewhat self-conscious liturgical enthusiast, anxious to participate as fully as possible in the public life of the Church, concentrates on joining in the responses to the Mass; while beside him kneels the old woman in a shawl, praying her rosary aloud and unmindful of the rest. The Gregorian Chant may flourish in one parish, while in the next, the old style 'Rosary, Sermon and Benediction' remains the Sunday afternoon standby of the faithful.

The school buildings, too, are visible reminders of change. There are still the small grimy buildings with inadequately partitioned classrooms; and the next parish puts up the square building of concrete and glass which has been the focus of the dreams, exhortations, and collections for so many years. Even while he is still unable to understand the issues involved, the young Catholic learns that he belongs to a religious minority which has fought for such schools and still often regards the demands to pay for them as unjust. He takes for granted so many things which strike the outsider as strange: the crucifixes and religious pictures, the prayers before and after lessons, and the moral sanctions on behaviour.

The new buildings are there beside the old. But what are the ideas and attitudes being communicated inside? If this study is concerned with a form of education which reaches only a section of the community, it is one of the most crucial. It has been stressed that Catholic grammar school education in the city is not a new phenomenon. Two of the schools were flourishing a hundred years ago. But in the past, comparatively few Catholics in the city went to such schools. The majority of those who attended them did so only because their parents could afford to pay for secondary education; they were the children of families who were either maintaining their social position or seeking to establish it through the traditional processes. It is true that a few went to such schools because they won scholarships; for them it represented a way of gaining status and of becoming more acceptable in the eyes of the wider society. But the very fact that they were so few made them all the more conscious of a sense of responsibility towards the Catholic community.

But what of the rapidly increasing numbers of young Catholics who would have been excluded in past years, and are now admitted in acordance with the provisions of the Butler Act? For them, as for others, grammar school education is still a way of learning and assimilating the values and way of living of the British middle classes. The Catholics may maintain separate schools, but they are based entirely upon this wider system. What are the consequences? It is certain that one cannot introduce large numbers of young people to this form of education without results which are important not only for them, but also for the society in which they live.

A little has been said of the vivid setting, sometimes a blending, and sometimes a tangle, of the traditional and the new, against which the young Catholics described in this survey grew up. To understand the views and behaviour of the former pupils of Catholic grammar schools in Liverpool, it is essential to remember the wider background which they all shared. The families and homes of those who were interviewed reveal in an individual context the changes taking place in the social structure of Catholicism in the city. Yet now their occupations are similar in status, showing how education has been instrumental in accelerating for some the processes of social mobility.

Individual Backgrounds

It remains now to consider in detail the individual backgrounds of those who were interviewed. Few came from large families, it may be noted, and as many as 14 per cent were only children.[1] Half of those who were interviewed came from families which had two or three children. Eighteen per cent of the families had four children; only 17 per cent of the families had more than four children. In the families of 80 per cent of those who were interviewed, both parents

1. See Floud, Halsey and Martin, *op. cit.*; also A. Anastasi, 'Intelligence and Family Size', *Psychological Bulletin*, 53 (1956), 187–206.

were living. In 5 per cent of the homes, the father only was living, and in another 15 per cent the mother alone was alive.

Because of the importance of employment as a guide in our society to a person's social class, it was originally planned to present a detailed analysis of parents' occupations. But the questions were, of course, addressed not to the parents themselves, but to their children. Thus, the ordinary difficulties of collecting accurate information on this were made even more complicated, for the answers included the usual wide terms such as 'engineer' and 'civil servant'. Other occupations were not named but were described in elaborate detail, such as that which began, 'He watches the cargo on the docks . . .' Clearly such descriptions had little meaning in terms of the Registrar General's classification of occupations. It was decided, therefore, that no attempt could be made to classify this information. The investigator was reluctant to pursue this point too far during the interviews, since some respondents may have very understandably wished to remain deliberately vague. Interestingly enough, the unskilled or manual trades were often stated clearly; answers included porters, lorry drivers, a commissionaire, a bill poster and dock labourers. Similarly, jobs at the other end of the scale, such as managerial positions, were described unambiguously. It was the clerical posts and factory jobs apparently involving supervisory functions which were sometimes hazily named.

In sharp contrast, the mothers' occupations were clearly described. Only 27 per cent of the mothers were employed. There were a few teachers, a couple who were self-employed, and a few who assisted in their husbands' businesses; these included two wives who worked in post offices and one in a public house. The remainder tended to work in shops, and cleaning jobs were mentioned occasionally. But it was interesting that out of the 95 per cent of the mothers still alive at the time of the inquiry, 68 per cent of the total were housewives—or as their children more often explained, 'Oh, she doesn't work.'

Within the families, the occupational range was often wide, and reflected the differences which education had introduced within the family circle. For instance, a young man who had just received a university degree came from a home where the father was a porter, a brother who had attended a grammar school was an electrical engineer, while another brother who had been to a secondary modern school was a lorry driver. Similarly, another young man's father was a docker; other members of the family were factory hands, while another brother was studying for the priesthood.

As one would expect in view of the differences between parents' occupations, the homes, too, varied enormously, ranging from large

detached or semi-detached houses in the more expensive suburbs,
through the new private housing estates, the City Corporation's old
and new housing areas, to tightly packed terraced houses in narrow
streets in the central districts and large blocks of flats in the same
areas. Some of those who were interviewed lived in the Crown Street
area which is being investigated by the Department of Social
Science.[1]

Family Education

Parents' education was regarded as important, indicating as it does
the changes between generations, and it was certainly easier to collect
information on this than on occupations. This revealed that as many
as 60 per cent came from homes where neither parent had attended
a grammar school. Although some could not recall the names of the
schools which their parents had last attended (this was true only of
those who had not been to grammar schools), all could give the
educational level with some degree of assurance. Table 3 shows the
small proportion coming from homes where both parents had
received a grammar school education.

TABLE 3

Education of Parents

Level of Parents' Education	Percentage of Respondents
Both parents with grammar school education	21
One parent with grammar school education	19
Neither parent with grammar school education	60

A few volunteered the information in answering this question that
a parent was not a Catholic or had become a Catholic after leaving
school, by way of explaining the fact that the school they had named
was not a Catholic one.[2]

But if few came from homes where both parents had received a
grammar school education, many more had brothers and sisters who
were attending or had attended grammar schools. Table 4 shows
this.

1. See J. B. Mays, 'Cultural Uniformity in Urban Areas: An Introduction to
the Crown Street Study in Liverpool', *The Sociological Review*, N.S., VI (1958),
95–108.
    2. The parents' religion was not asked for at any point, for this might have
involved embarrassment.

TABLE 4

Education of Other Members of the Family

Education of Siblings	Percentage of Respondents
One or more siblings receiving, or having received grammar school education	70
Siblings not receiving or having received grammar school education	15
Not applicable	14

Ethnic Origin

Although the families and homes were different in so many respects, there was something which many of these young people had in common: ethnic origin. It was particularly noticeable that a high proportion of surnames revealed the Irish origin of the father's family. Table 5 reveals the ethnic origin of the families, and shows that few were of English, or even British origin. Several families had come from the Continent, including Eastern Europe. Many people replied to the question about their family's origin in a way which indicated that the answer was superfluous. Evidently, many still regarded Catholicism in Liverpool as being synonymous with an Irish origin, and most regarded it as self-evident that their families should have originated there. This appeared to be taken for granted, although a defensive pride was sometimes implied in their answers, finding its outlet in a joking remark, such as 'All our disreputable ancestors came from Ireland!' Several respondents had one or both parents who were actually born in Ireland, while one girl was herself Irish born. The majority, however, belonged to families who had lived in Liverpool for at least one generation

The young people who were interviewed, then, came from settled families by and large. It seems that most had grown accustomed to the idea that they still had connections with ways of life which had originated outside this country, and it is a pity that questions were not asked about this. It would be interesting, too, to see if such people later reject their ethnic origins as they become further assimilated into the middle classes. There is often a distinct prestige element that is attached by English Catholics to belonging to families which remained Catholic during the Reformation. Perhaps this means that those who become socially mobile will be anxious to cut themselves off from what is, after all, a peasant tradition. In Liverpool at the present time, however, there does not seem to be much reaction against it, and the writer can remember vividly that while she was at school, almost everybody (including Philippinos, it may be said) wore shamrock on St. Patrick's Day, although no encouragement to do so was given by the school, and hardly anyone had been born in Ireland.

TABLE 5

Ethnic Origin of the Family

Origin of Family	Percentage of Respondents
Predominantly Irish	46
Irish on one side	25
Irish and European	5
European	5
Other non-United Kingdom	2
United Kingdom	13
Did not know	4

Such, then, were the different social backgrounds from which the former pupils came; the only factor, apart from Catholicism, which was present in most being that the family was not of British origin.

Respondents' Education

The educational experiences of the respondents before going to a grammar school seemed to reflect, by and large, the differences in their economic circumstances, although occasionally a child from a working class home had been given a private education. Nearly half, 46 per cent, had attended the schools attached to their own parishes immediately prior to going to a secondary school. This was a considerable advantage in analyzing the material, since it was possible to compare the behaviour and attitudes of those who had attended their parochial schools with that of those who had not. As Table 6 shows, the schools attended by those who were interviewed varied considerably. The information about earlier schools, where this was applicable, is even more complex. Many had attended several schools, for the situation was complicated by the fact that all those interviewed had started attending school during the second World War when some had been evacuated to rural areas or had lived with their grandparents or other relatives.

As many as 34 per cent had been educated in a private Catholic school before going to a grammar school; for the majority, this had

TABLE 6

Education Prior to Grammar School

Schools attended prior to grammar schools	Percentage of Respondents
Own parochial school	46
Parochial school other than own	11
Private Roman Catholic school	4
Private Roman Catholic school attached to school subsequently attended	30
Local authority primary school	4
Other school	6

meant the preparatory department of the school subsequently attended. It was noticeable that few had gone to non-Catholic schools of any sort, although two or three had lived on a new housing estate where there was no Catholic school at that time and so had been to a local authority primary school.

Respondents' Occupations

In spite of these differences in family circumstances and early educational experiences, the years spent at a grammar school resulted in the majority preparing for professional occupations, as Table 7 shows. Most had undertaken further study or training of some sort. Nearly half were either studying at university at the time they were interviewed, or else had just completed their course, not all successfully. Only a quarter of the university students were living away from home, a point which is of importance in considering their behaviour and attitudes. It was Liverpool University which attracted most of them, although at least two of the schools strongly discouraged this.

In addition, a substantial proportion were or had been students at Catholic Teacher Training Colleges and subsequently taught or intended to teach in Catholic schools. Only two of these were young men, one of whom had done his National Service before going to college. Quite a few of the girls had attended a local college, although they had been resident during term. The remainder had studied at places as far afield as Hull and Newcastle. Attendance at such colleges means that as far as their work was concerned most had been associated with other Catholics ever since they had left school.

A few more were students at other colleges, and one who had just finished a three year course away from Liverpool was about to teach. There were a few young men who were student apprentices

TABLE 7

Respondents' Occupations

Occupations	Percentage of Respondents
University Students:	
Liverpool	30
Manchester, living in Liverpool	4
Other	12
Teachers in Catholic Schools	27
Other teachers	1
Students at Catholic Training Colleges	2
Students at other colleges	4
Student apprentices	7
Other sorts of training	6
Other occupations	7

with industrial firms. One of these had been a university student for a time, but had been sent down after failing his examinations. Several others had undertaken some sort of training for a profession, such as accountancy. Of the remainder, one was a housewife. The others fitted into no precise category. Several had held a variety of jobs since leaving school; one young man, for example, had left university after failing his examinations, and at the time of the fieldwork he was a factory labourer. Only two of the men had been in the Forces.

Almost all, then, had undertaken some further study or training. A handful had been unsuccessful, but most were either professionally qualified or on their way to being so. For them, grammar school education was the preliminary rather than the final step in their careers. Without it, they would probably not have been able to take up the careers they had chosen.

Thus, most had chosen occupations which continued to restrict the amount of time at their disposal after leaving school. Moreover, some were away from Liverpool during term, and a few were intending to take employment away from the city when they had completed their training. Lest these be overestimated, however, it must be said that most were firmly rooted in Liverpool. It was clear from the interviews and observation that their friendships and interests, as well as their homes, were still closely linked with the city. Another important consequence of the careers they had chosen was that wage earning had been deferred for two, three, or even more years. It is hardly surprising, therefore, then, that only two, one of each sex, were married at the time they were interviewed.

All had left school for three years at the time of the fieldwork, and the ages of those who were interviewed did not vary widely. The majority were in their early twenties, although one girl was as young as nineteen. It is noticeable that the boys tended to be a little older than the girls. This is partly accounted for by the fact that more of the former stayed on to the Sixth Form for a third year.[1]

So even though their social origins were very different, grammar school education has enabled most of these young people to enter occupations which enjoy a high status in our society. Some were following in their fathers' footsteps, but others have made a considerable jump in the social hierarchy. What consequences does this have for them? And for Catholicism in the city? The following chapters try to find some of the answers to these questions, and thus trace some of the changes taking place in Liverpool Catholicism which are not so strikingly apparent as the new schools and churches springing up.

1. This matter is complicated even further by the policy which two of the boys' schools had of moving pupils into the Sixth Form as early as possible to allow them to spend three years there.

Chapter 4

RELIGIOUS VIEWS

IN the previous chapter, the cultural setting of those who were interviewed was sketched in, and the section of society to which they belonged was briefly described. It is also important to consider them from another angle; to study their ideas, and the way they react to situations, or, in other words, to examine them as individuals rather than as a group in society. Some attention must be given to their attitudes towards religion in general, to determine how far they accepted the beliefs of Catholicism, and what they thought membership of the Catholic Church meant.

It is clearly very difficult to find answers to such questions, since one quickly finds oneself trying to assess the relationship between values and behaviour. In view of the obvious difficulties, it is hardly surprising that by far the greater part of contemporary research in the sociology of religion has confined itself to the study of attendance at Mass, baptismal records, the numbers of religious vocations, and other indications of the religious life in an area. Such data have the double advantage of being reasonably easy to obtain and of being acceptable indications of behaviour. No one can quibble at the results of a census of people at a service, provided it is properly carried out. As a result, the study of attitudes has largely been left to the field of social psychology, where such investigations are numerous.[1] But confining sociological inquiries to the measurement of religious practice and similar matters means that the results can only be descriptive,[2] demonstrating that a particular behaviour pattern exists in a certain area. Why this should be so then remains a matter for speculation. What is needed is an approach of a more strictly sociological nature which will try to understand behaviour in its social context, with particular reference to the attitudes associated with any behaviour patterns that may be found to exist. At the present stage, such an inquiry in the sphere of religious behaviour can only be tentative in the extreme, and in describing the results of this section of the inquiry, the limitations of the material collected must be borne in mind. Were the investigation to be repeated, there are

1. Some have been referred to in Chapter 1; see also the very interesting studies which have appeared in *Lumen Vitae*.
2. Cf. the comments on the inadequacy of superficial studies of religious factors in S. S. Acquaviva, *L'eclissi del sacro nella civiltà industriale*, Milan, 1961, especially p. 20.

sections of this study which would be expanded because the findings have shown how promising these areas are; there are others which would be excluded because their inclusion served little evident purpose.

Church Attendance

However important the study of attitudes may be in the analysis of religious behaviour, the great emphasis placed by the Catholic Church upon attendance at church means that this cannot be dismissed lightly in studying a group of Catholics. All baptized Catholics reaching the age of reason (usually considered to be about seven years of age) are bound by Canon Law to attend Mass on Sundays, and to make their Easter duties, that is, to receive Communion about Easter time. A good deal of thought, therefore, was given to this. The problem in the present investigation with regard to church attendance was two-fold. On the one hand, would answers to questions about religious practice achieve anything other than an expression of what those who were interviewed thought was desirable? No matter how truthful people may wish to be in discussing such matters, there is usually a tendency to speak in terms of what one intends to do, rather than what one actually does.

The other aspect of the problem was more serious, and it was this which was ultimately responsible for the final decision to omit questions about religious observance. Preliminary interviews made it clear that to include such matters would prejudice the success of the entire fieldwork. Such a difficulty might have been predicted in relation to Catholics who did not attend church, and who might, in view of the Church's emphasis on this, feel resentful or guilty if they were questioned about it. But the crux of the issue was revealed in the course of the preliminary interviews with university students who were observed to attend Mass frequently during the week, that is, who chose to do more than to fulfil the Church's minimum obligations. They were very willing to answer questions on other matters, including those on religious beliefs; but when the topic of religious practice was brought up, objections were made by some that such inquiries were an intrusion into a private realm, a view with which many will sympathize.[1] In speaking of religious opinions, a respondent can give an evasive or ambiguous answer without embarrassment; attendance at church cannot be dealt with in this way, for a direct reply is required. Although many of those interviewed in the preliminary stages did not make this point, it was evident that to make inquiries of this kind involved too great a risk.

1. It must be remembered that the Continental work on this has involved censuses of people actually present in church, not on reported behaviour.

However, the problem of obtaining information about religious observance was not so difficult as might be supposed. By and large, those who were interviewed seemed to fall into two categories, one considerably larger than the other. The first consisted of the majority who appeared to take the matter of church attendance for granted, and referred to it casually as they talked. While this was useful, the questions were carefully phrased so that anyone who no longer attended church, and who wished to conceal the fact, was not embarrassed.[1] The other category consisted of a small handful who either rejected the Catholic Church's teaching in general, or who were doubtful about its validity. These were surprisingly ready to talk, and only one of all those encountered during the fieldwork refused to answer a question of this kind. Thus, the major religious issue with those who were interviewed was not so much whether they attended church, but whether or not they accepted the beliefs of Catholicism. If they believed, they went to church; for them the matter was as simple as this. There were no signs at any point of the different attitude reported by investigators in other *milieux*, that one accepted Catholic beliefs after a fashion and certainly one was baptized, married, and wished to be interred according to Catholic custom, but for the rest did not bother too much about fulfilling the obligations of church attendance. The respondents in the present study had a good deal to say about this attitude, which they criticized severely.

On the other hand, the converse way of thinking, that if one did not believe, one did not go to church, did not necessarily apply. One young man, for instance, went to church to conceal from his family the fact that he was an agnostic, to save hurting them. In the present investigation, the numbers of those who did not believe or who were uncertain of the validity of Catholicism were so small that it is difficult to draw many conclusions from their answers. Clearly they represent an interesting section, and if the present study is anything to go by, they are not so reticent in such matters as one might expect. Given the right circumstances, they appear to be ready to state their views freely.

The questions on religious beliefs were deliberately introduced in the middle of the interview, to allow time for respondents to relax. Questions on the Sixth Form religious lessons led up to them;[2] views on the religious lessons had in fact already revealed a good deal with regard to opinions on religion, as earlier answers on the schools and

1. Cf. the wording of the question on church attendance in Ward, *op. cit.*, p. 50, '*If you go to Mass*, do you go to different churches or to the same church always?' (Italics not in original.)
2. As the Sixth Form experiences are not directly relevant to the investigation, they will be described elsewhere later.

the former pupils' associations had done. It was particularly noticeable that in talking about the Sixth Form lessons, the majority identified themselves very decidedly with Catholicism. The fierce criticisms of religious education made by some usually contained an appeal to the ideals they accepted. Thus, the topic of religious beliefs was introduced easily into the context of these remarks, and it was noticeable how freely and readily the majority replied. In fact, in view of this willingness to co-operate, the investigator would probably be ready to ask far more questions on this if the survey were repeated.[1]

Changes in Others' Religious Ideas

First, those who were interviewed were asked whether they thought other people changed their views on religion after leaving school. However, in spite of this deliberately oblique approach, the personal element was very evident in many replies. Some referred to their own experiences immediately. For instance, a young man who had changed his views drastically commented, 'Quite definitely. It depends on what happens. I can only speak from my own experiences. I went up from school with a friend, and he shares my views.' Others, however, answered in less personal terms and related stories to the interviewer of people whom they knew, usually friends from school, in an attempt to describe how people could change their religious views. Although the question was left deliberately wide, nearly all replied in terms of those who had received a similar education, and almost invariably referred to Catholics only.

Eighteen per cent could not think of ways in which people changed their views about religion, and a few more said they did not know about others, usually adding a personal comment, such as, 'I don't know about people in general. *I* have to a certain extent. I'm more aware of the problems that other people face, and that we face in trying to help them. It's not all so cut and dried as it once was.' Another person remarked, 'I suppose people do. They must cease to be convinced because they leave [the Church]. I can't say I know anyone who has gone that way.'

The remainder of the answers described the ways in which people change their views on religion, but the analysis of such replies was made particularly difficult by their complexity, since most suggested more than one. Certain elements, however, can be distinguished. Nearly a quarter of the answers referred to Catholics becoming more critical towards their beliefs as a result of contact with those who

1. A similar readiness to co-operate is reported by other investigators in this field, e.g. De Volder, *loc. cit.*, and J. Byrne, *A Study of Student Problems in Catholic Men's Colleges*, Washington, 1957.

did not share them. Such replies indicated the difficulties young Catholics might encounter after they left an environment largely composed of people with similar ideas, to move in a wider environment. Another important point which emerged was that a higher value was placed by them upon the faith of those who had experienced a period of questioning.

Examples of this sort of reply were:

You meet people who come up with problems. Sometimes it alters your own views on religion. Sometimes a person's faith weakens, but sometimes it's strengthened. You begin to search. It's a testing point, standing on your own feet.

Yes, I think so. Well, at school, you accepted everything everybody told you. When you leave, you have doubts. You weigh things up and see why you believe them, not just because you're told in class.

Mm, everybody—well, most people—go through a spell of seeing the other side of the picture from the one they've been taught. They begin to question blind acceptance and compare what they believe with other religions.

Yes, they think about it seriously for the first time and come into contact with non-Catholics. You're bound to change and start questioning things, especially at university, and look for reasons.

Some referred in their answers to Catholics either becoming more interested in their faith or losing interest altogether. One person voiced this opinion by saying, 'People either improve greatly or drop off. It all depends on the company you go with. You think more. You just jog along at school.' Another put it this way: 'It depends on the individual and the influences they come into contact with . . . there's no in-between stage. I think they either go one way or the other.'

A few suggested that the changes which took place lay in attitudes towards religion. The process was thus described by one young man:

Whether or not you change your basic ideas, you certainly change your attitude. At school, there's not much argument or thought. It's part of your life and it's accepted to a large extent. Our Sixth Form religious teacher tried to snap us out of this, but a lot of schools are the other way. If you meet someone who can put ideas better, it can wreck your confidence.

In 30 per cent of the answers there was reference to some Catholics either losing interest in their religion or rejecting it altogether. A student apprentice, for example, answered:

Yes, as soon as they leave school, 50 per cent aren't interested any more. Once the influence of the school has gone, it's up to yourself more or less. Quite a few I've met have said, 'I don't bother any more.'

References of this sort to known individuals were often made, as was the case, for instance, with the student who said:

Definitely. I've heard about one person from our school who's an agnostic now. He always was prone to argue. If he's following his own conscience, that's fair enough. I suppose when you're young you take a lot of what teachers and priests say on faith. Later on you want to be sure it's reasonable.

Great emphasis was placed in the replies upon the impact of environmental factors upon religious beliefs. A typical answer of this sort, coming from a university student, was:

It all depends on what they do after they leave. If they're in constant contact with the Church, I don't think their basic ideas will change at all. If they drift away, their ideas *will* change. They'll think it's a whole great fairy story. It depends on the will. If you're weak-willed, you'll be led anywhere.

Twelve per cent of the replies suggested that after leaving school, people became much more tolerant in their approach towards the beliefs of other people.

Changes in Personal Religious Ideas

Very similar sorts of answers were given when people described how they had changed their ideas, although the emphasis shifted in replying to this question. More, for instance, thought that they had not changed their views at all since leaving school. Fifty-eight per cent did not think their views on religion were basically any different, whereas only 18 per cent had thought other people did not change theirs. Typical examples of replies from the former were:

I'm not aware of any. I suppose one does change without being able to see. I don't think so. I always feel I could never miss Mass. I only do the necessary things, but I couldn't miss, even when I was in the Forces and on holidays.

Some who had said immediately that they had not changed their basic beliefs then went on to make comments or reservations. A fifth of the answers described how people had grown more interested in Catholicism and found it more important and relevant to their lives after leaving school. One person said slowly, 'No, I don't think I have', then added, 'I *understand* it more; I think more of it since I left school—so I *have* changed!' A young teacher remarked:

Yes, by going to training college, I mixed with people from other Catholic grammar schools. They seemed to have a better Catholic education than me. By training for teaching, it began to mean more. We—the people from our school—realized how little we knew—basic stuff we should have known.

A similar reply, from a university student this time, was:

Yes, when I was at school I didn't take religion seriously. I went to church and I said my prayers. But now I don't go to church as often as I used to, but religion is now much more personal. I realize it's a serious matter.

Another fifth said that they were more tolerant in their attitude towards others. One girl said briefly, 'I don't think I have really. I'm more mellow, that's all.' Other examples were:

I haven't changed, but I'm more ready to sympathize with different ideas. My convictions are still fundamentally the same.

I've always held these things on faith. I'm beginning to see the reason for many of them. I'm less dogmatic in my approach. I used to snap down on arguments. Now I can see where they all fall down.

Only in so far as I've unbent a little more. I'm more tolerant.

In 13 per cent of the answers there were references to a more critical attitude towards Catholicism. One girl, for instance, answered, 'Not the basic ideas. I have doubts about things—but right inside I know I'm wrong.' A young man replied, 'Towards the basic principles, I still agree—yes, I think I still agree with them. There are two points I'm not clear about the Catholic viewpoint.' He then elaborated in great detail his two points of disagreement. Both were concerned with the moral teaching of the Catholic Church. One was a point of view popularly attributed to the Church but is in fact contrary to Catholic teaching. He then attempted to draw the interviewer into argument, showing strong resentment at her unwillingness to do so.

A handful described how they had experienced a period of doubt or indifference, which was followed by increased interest and appreciation. A teacher, for instance, answered, 'Fundamentally, I don't think so. You get a phase at college, but I got over that. Now I'm teaching, I've got a far greater love of my religion. You can't give what you haven't got yourself.'

Similar replies came from two university students:

I was very lax at university. I went to Mass every week, that's all. I was going round with atheists and I got the impression that to have a religion was to be in a minority of one. Then I met a Catholic who was living a far better life than me. That made me feel ashamed and made me practise with more fervour.

Not basically. I did go through a period in first year, a doubting period— you know. I never gave up going to church, but I often wished the Church was more flexible. I know now it can't be, but it's very difficult to explain.

None of the answers made reference to having less interest in religion after leaving school, although, as has been pointed out, some were more critical. Amongst these were two girls whose doubts about the credibility of Catholicism were more strongly expressed than the others, and their views did not imply, as the others had done (if not in answer to that question, then in reply to others), that they were still practising Catholics. One of them said:

I believe a good deal less now, but I wasn't very strong at school. It's just in general. I always had doubts about the Catholic faith. I was never answered very satisfactorily. I don't move in Catholic circles to support my ideas. I've heard more convincing viewpoints. I wouldn't say I didn't believe. I'm more in a quandary . . . I don't think it's because I left school, it's just a natural development.

The other's answer was very similar:

I don't know what I believe at the moment. For one thing, the biggest shock I got was that a lot of non-Catholics are just as firm in their views. The Catholic religion is so controversial that you have to question it every day. I question everything. I don't think my belief in God has changed, but differences in religion seem very petty.

A third young women had this to say about the way she had changed her religious views:

Oh, yes, entirely. When I've thrashed it out, I'll probably become quite convinced.

Two young men made it clear, one of them from the outset, that they no longer regarded themselves as Catholics. One of them, a university student, remarked:

I just haven't got any faith. It means nothing to me now. I vaguely believe in God. The environmental influences are very strong. If I was knocked down, I would probably ask for a priest. I go to church every Sunday when I'm home. The family doesn't know.

The other young man had this to say:

Drastically. I'm still changing. I'm no longer a practising Catholic, but I'm sympathetic to the Catholic religion, whereas I was at one time anti-pathetic to it.

The only members of his family attending church were two young children, but the living room contained several religious pictures.

Another two young men answered ambiguously that they had changed their views since leaving school, but the direction of that change was left vague. One was reported by his friend to be no longer a practising Catholic. A third young man said:

I haven't changed my ideas. I'm more critical, as I say. Do you mind if I leave that one over? I have some problems here.

This was the only refusal. In the case of ambiguous answers on this topic, the interviewer did not press for clarification. This was a particularly intimate area, and gratitude for the generous way in which people co-operated made the interviewer all the more reluctant to inquire further when vague answers were given.

There were, then, few who were willing to reject Catholic beliefs explicitly at this stage. Although there were some who experienced difficulties in accepting the doctrines of the Church, most of these people expressed the idea that eventually these difficulties would smooth themselves out. They regarded them rather in the light of growing pains, a necessary part in the maturing of one's faith.

Validity of the Replies

The question must now be faced, how valid are such replies? Did people say what they thought was expected of them rather than what they really believed? There were two checks applied to the validity of these responses. Firstly, there was that of internal consistency within the interviews. Although a few were guarded, understandably, in their answers to this particular question, most replied very freely, and the views were remarkably consistent with those expressed in reply to questions where an indirect approach was made. It is, of course, possible that some may have set out systematically to mislead the interviewer in this regard; however, the length and scope of the interview made this somewhat unlikely. The answers were by no means monosyllabic, and to maintain a pretence successfully would have been a remarkable feat. Most expounded their ideas on religion for a considerable period of time.

The second check on validity gives even firmer confirmation: those who were interviewed often spoke of friends whose religious views had changed. Without identification being sought in any way by the investigator, the fact that they were usually people from the same form at school made this inevitable as a rule, although respondents were not always aware of this. In any case, the same individuals were often referred to anonymously in several interviews. Sometimes after an interview, people would ask if the investigator had seen a particular person. When the interviewer stated again that the names of those taking part were confidential, the explanation was given that the name had been suggested because the person concerned had 'interesting' or 'funny' views on religion.

In only two instances was there any inconsistency. The two young men who rejected Catholicism entirely each reported that he had a friend who shared his views to some extent. One of them was a young man who had answered ambiguously. The other remarked:

I haven't changed any basic ideas, but I've looked at others' viewpoints, and looked for answers, and I'm less complacent.

Throughout the interview, his replies reflected strong identification with Catholic values, particularly when he gave his views on why Catholics stopped going to church.

Study of Religion

Other attitudes towards religion were displayed when the question was asked if Catholics had any need to study their religion after

leaving school, and the reasons why. It was expected that the majority
would automatically reply in the affirmative, but that their reasons
might contain some useful information. Eighty-two per cent, composed of an equal number of girls and boys, considered that more
study was necessary. The replies emphasized the inadequacy at a
later age of the knowledge of Catholicism gained at school. One
girl commented:

Yes, you have to keep learning more about it so as to maintain interest in
it. You should broaden the basis learned at school. That's rather idealistic.
I haven't done it myself. It has to be personal.

A similar remark was:

Yes, because as you're progressing with everything else, you should progress with religion. *I* haven't done anything about it. An awful lot don't
know things they should have learned in school. I'm awfully stupid in discussion.

Another person even went so far as to say, 'I don't think you've
studied it *before* you've left school'.

Frequent references were made to the necessity of studying in
order to be able to discuss religious matters intelligently and to
answer questions on Catholicism. Many lamented their own inadequacy in this respect, as the following replies indicate:

Mm, you forget a great deal of what you've learned earlier on, and you get
asked various sides of religion you've never thought about.
I think they could do with it. I know *I* could do with it. I could crawl into
a corner when I'm asked questions.
Definitely, definitely. Most of them—a great many—seem to forget what
they've learned. *Me*, for instance! When you're in factories, there are lots
of non-Catholics . . . All these ideas have an effect. You tend to get rather
lax. You should study the things you come up against every day, questions
you get asked. But in the forefront of one's mind should be the importance
of going to Mass and the sacraments.

Most thought that Catholics should study their religion 'in general',
with special attention to the questions put to them by those with
whom they worked or studied; as one remarked:

Yes, definitely, because you're coming into contact with people who are
not Catholics. You should study the dogmas and the Creed and find about
these first, before you start on little questions. Many Catholics are too concerned with pious practices.

Some thought that discussion groups starting with a talk would be
a helpful means of studying Catholicism, but most stressed the need
for tackling questions about which individuals found they had a need
to discover more. However, it is doubtful if these proposals were
anything more than a matter of form in most cases. The majority

spontaneously admitted that they did not study their faith them-selves. There are several groups in Liverpool, such as the Catholic Evidence Guild, the Newman Association and the Catholic Social Guild, which already offer facilities of the sort proposed in the inter-views. The answers seem to indicate notional assent only to the ideal of continuing to study one's religion. They reveal, moreover, the danger of collecting proposals for new projects without considering how far the facilities already in existence are used.

Twelve per cent did not consider further study necessary. A typical answer was, 'No, you're taught enough in school. You should just put it into practice.' A similar comment from a university student was, 'I don't think so. Maybe people who go to elementary schools don't cover sufficient ground. But they do in grammar schools.' One or two replied in terms of 'If they want to'.

Why Catholics Stop Going to Church

In giving their views as to why Catholics stopped going to church, much of what has been said already was confirmed. Many told the interviewer of someone they knew, but it was sometimes difficult to decide whether the replies were the result of experience or were simply speculation. However, this is not particularly important for the present purposes; the question was primarily designed to elicit attitudes towards church-going. Moreover, it is worth remembering Pin's comment that the Catholic who believes and practises his religion is potentially an unbeliever, and as such can understand why others do not believe. He also points out that since it is difficult to obtain a frank reply from those who do not believe, and par-ticularly from those who do not practise, it is probable, in his opinion, that the practising Catholic will be able to describe more adequately the reasons for lack of belief and practice.[1]

The difficulties over belief, which some reported experiencing shortly after leaving school, would lead one to expect that the major reasons given for Catholics ceasing to attend church would be con-cerned with doubts about the validity of Catholicism. It is surprising, therefore, to see how few in fact gave this as a factor and how unsym-pathetic the majority of the replies were. Only a handful gave diffi-culties in matters of faith as the sole suggestion, although several more included this with other reasons. Examples were:

Lack of belief in the Catholic faith, I think, with university students. There are so many things in the Catholic religion that you have to accept and can't reason out. They can't understand these things. They feel there's no point in going.

1. *Op cit.*, p. 267. Chapter 10 in this study by Pin contains the results of an investigation on the question of loss of faith.

Most of them I know say they've thought it all over. They tend to be a bit sceptical, because they don't take up another religion. It varies from person to person. In a lot of cases, it's just a habit from school and being in Catholic homes. They stop going to church as soon as they get away.

Although few gave only one reason, the predominating response was that laziness and indifference were the main reasons for people ceasing to attend church. Such answers showed attitudes of rejection towards Catholics who no longer went to church. As many as 40 per cent included laziness in their answers, most giving it as their first suggestion, as the following illustrations show:

Laziness more than anything. Then they try to convince themselves it's a lot of hooey, trying to cover up their laziness.

Laziness is the main thing. Also being fairly weak-willed. Then they're influenced by the strong-willed. I'm convinced that laziness is at the bottom. Also, if they're away from home, there's no one to remind them. Some have a simple faith and don't think of reasons and are inclined to give up, too.

Laziness. Moral laziness is, I suppose, the greater. Going to church indicates some bowing down to authority. If you bow down on Sunday, you must bow down during the week when you don't want to. If you don't go on Sunday, you can forget during the week. It's much more convenient to forget. I suppose that's the main reason. Very few Catholics stop because of convictions that God doesn't exist. It's just pure laziness as far as I know.

Similar replies were given by those who gave indifference as the main factor, as 17 per cent did. Like the parishioners of St. Catherine's, they emphasized that people stopped going gradually rather than making a deliberate decision not to go.[1] This can be seen in the following extracts:

I think it's purely and simply that they get into an attitude of couldn't-care-less. I don't think they say, 'I'm not going.' It's just a gradual falling off. They don't give any thought to it—that's the problem. They've that many other things to do that religion takes about tenth place in their lives.

The main reason is because they can't be bothered getting up on Sundays. It's easier now with evening Masses. They leave it, then something else crops up. I don't think they think about it. I've never met anyone who made a decision.

Environmental factors came into 41 per cent of the answers. Sometimes such replies revealed hostile or defensive attitudes towards the environment in which those who were interviewed worked or studied. They showed, too, that these young Catholics often found it hard to maintain minority beliefs, and, like the answers to other questions of this sort, illustrate how they saw themselves as distinct from the community at large because of these beliefs. The

1. Ward, *op. cit.*, p. 151.

importance of the company one kept was frequently referred to in the answers. One person summed up the point about environmental factors by saying succinctly, 'Because they meet someone that doesn't go'. Others had this to say:

I think their religion has never meant enough to them. They've never thought about it. They've taken a lot for granted. I suppose we're spoonfed. You leave school and you're on your own. They get so caught up with things. If they go to university, with leading a university life, they tend to overlook religion.

Well, I should say mainly because on leaving school, they're mixing with non-Catholics. They haven't someone behind them. Even if you're not paying attention to the religious lessons, they're there, aren't they?

I don't know. I suppose mixing more with non-Catholic people. There's a certain discipline at school. People know you and criticize you. There's freedom after you've left school.

Only one person suggested moral problems as the sole reason, but it was included in 18 per cent of the answers. This was a category of reply which tended to be more sympathetic than the others. An example of a reply including this point was:

I suppose confession is quite a good reason. They have to confess things and are afraid to, or know they'll do it again. Another, I suppose, is just not having—[pause]—I think religion clicks with you at some point in your life. You come to value it. If it doesn't, then you stop. And I think living by oneself away from Catholic homes makes a lot of difference. Perhaps meeting people who argue if you're not convinced yourself.

Only one person suggested that it was resentment which caused people to stay away from church. This young man remarked:

I think it's usually personal resentment against someone. My father stopped because of an argument with the priest. Another member of the family stopped because of going with a Protestant. They did not get a dispensation, so they got married in a Registry Office.

A handful suggested that some stopped going to church in reaction against religious teaching in school. There were only a few who said they had never met anyone who did not go.

Thus, with the exception of those who attributed ceasing to go to church to lack of belief, and some of those who believed moral difficulties were the cause, the views of the majority strongly rejected Catholics who stopped practising their religion. A university student who made this rejection explicit had this to say:

Quite honestly, I think it's a form of conceit when it comes to Catholics leaving school and going to university. They think they're being clever giving up. I think very few can possibly be sincere.

In view of the frank way in which those who were interviewed spoke of their own difficulties, it was surprising how few were sympathetic towards those who left the Church. Their answers emphasized that to be a Catholic was difficult and left one in the minority. It is not surprising that such replies usually came from university students and those working in industry. A student apprentice, for example, commented:

I suppose some are lazy. Others can't be bothered. They don't *feel* any different, so they don't bother. If they mix with non-Catholics, they think they're better off as non-Catholics. It definitely makes you different from other people being a Catholic. I suppose some don't like that. I know a couple who feel they'd be more popular if they weren't Catholics.

Similarly, a university student with friends who no longer went to church, after suggesting other reasons, added:

With others, it's sheer egoism. Some of them, when they go to university, become carried away by the sense of their own importance. They become little dictators. They're influenced by shallow arguments.

Conclusions

Thus, most considered ceasing to attend church as a severe defection from the norms of behaviour they accepted. The majority attributed it to laziness, indifference, or succumbing to unfavourable environmental influences. This confirmed the attitudes they had already expressed in describing their own beliefs. Although a few no longer believed or else had severe doubts about the credibility of Catholic doctrine, the majority stated that being a Catholic meant far more to them now, than it had while they were at school.[1] In some ways, they were more ready to come to terms with their environment than they had been at school, expressing a better understanding of the beliefs of others and a greater willingness to believe such people were sincere.

But in other ways, they clearly saw themselves as a distinct group which had to maintain its beliefs and values in the face of opposition. They emphasized the importance of these values to their lives, and stressed the necessity of accepting them on rational grounds rather than because they had been taught to hold them. In the light of this way of thinking, their criticism of Catholics who do not consider their faith seriously and so cease to go to church becomes explicable. Their rejecting attitude towards such people is an indication of how important they considered Catholicism. The statements of opinion in this section were generally more clear-cut than those made in other parts of the interview. The views towards groups within the Catholic Church, which will be described later, often made the point that such activities were there for those who wanted them. Their opinions on the beliefs of the Catholic Church, on the other hand, were usually stated uncompromisingly.

1. Cf. A. Godin, 'La fonction symbolique', *Lumen Vitae*, X, 2 (1955), 298–310.

Whatever the limitations of information obtained by the methods of direct inquiry, it is at least clear that it is possible to obtain statements of belief and opinion in this way. While such statements must necessarily be viewed with caution, they have their uses, in that behaviour becomes far more explicable against the background of such attitudes. The fact that some information can be gained in this way is an encouragement to advance in research from the preliminary level of the consideration of factors such as church attendance.

Here, then, is an outline of how a section of young Catholics described their opinions and attitudes towards religious beliefs. Up to now, most attitude studies have stopped, tantalizingly, at this point. Yet it is here that the most important part of the analysis begins. It has been shown that most of those who were interviewed said that they accepted the beliefs of the Roman Catholic Church and considered that their behaviour was influenced by them. What were the consequences of these beliefs? What part did the acceptance of Catholic beliefs lead them to play in the social groupings of the Church? After the next chapter has considered the influence of the school community, an attempt will be made to describe some of the social consequences of these beliefs.

Chapter 5

THE SCHOOL COMMUNITY

MENTION has already been made of the fact that those who were interviewed came from nine grammar schools, all of them day schools at the time. They differ from one another in their organization,[1] but are similar in most important aspects. All allot some, if not all, of their places to pupils who are not required to pay fees, though some admitted applicants who had passed the schools' own entrance examination and paid fees. The schools themselves vary in age, location and appearance. More than one is over a hundred years old, whilst another is a completely new building on the outskirts of the city.[2] The surroundings range from pleasant, mellowed buildings set in their own grounds, to two convents whose severe façades look out on to the city's busy streets; even these, however, guard their own beautifully kept gardens behind the houses, to astonish visitors with the unexpected.

The head teachers of all the nine schools are members of religious orders and congregations.[3] Most of the teachers, however, are lay people. The most recently opened grammar school in Liverpool, referred to in Chapter 2, comes under the Archdiocese of Liverpool, and the headmaster is a member of the secular clergy.

The writer's own experience led her to formulate the hypothesis that the stress upon the grammar school as a social community would have important consequences for the social life of the Catholic Church in Liverpool. Having attended one of these schools, she was aware that a dominant part was played by the school in the lives of the pupils. This was not simply a matter of lessons and of study, for there were religious organizations, dramatic societies, debates, activities which were all important in influencing attitudes towards life. Above all, there was the question of friendship. The concentration of attention upon school life leaves little time for the maturing of early friendships with children of the neighbourhood, and there

1. One boys' school and three girls' schools are aided grammar schools. Two boys' schools and two girls' schools are direct grant grammar schools, and one girls' school is independent.
2. Since the fieldwork was carried out, another school has moved its premises to the outskirts of the city.
3. See E. K. Francis, 'Towards a Typology of Religious Orders', *American Journal of Sociology*, LV, 5 (1950), 437–49. Also, H. P. M. Goddijn, 'The Sociology of Religious Orders and Congregations', *Social Compass*, VII, 5–6 (1960), 431–47.

are no real opportunities to develop new relationships outside the school context. Obviously, one does have friends who do not attend the same school, but the intimate contact which one has with school fellows is lacking. How far was this true of the former pupils of Catholic grammar schools in general?[1]

The whole inquiry hinges upon the role played in the lives of young Catholics by the grammar school as a social institution. It was soon evident from interviews with headteachers that the way of life of the schools extended far beyond the activities which were more strictly concerned with the pupils' studies. Interviews with the former pupils revealed that for most of them the school was not just a building where they received their lessons. For many, it was the most important reference group for a substantial, and a formative, period of their lives. It had a tremendous impact on what they did with their leisure time, and with whom that time was spent. In the sphere of religion, too, it played a very dominant role.

Since the main theme of this study is concerned with changes in the social groupings within the Catholic Church, it is interesting to see that one of the consequences of the growing importance of grammar school education is that functions more usually associated with the parish have been transferred to the grammar schools. There are two particularly noticeable ways in which this has happened. Firstly, the priest responsible for the spiritual welfare of the pupils is now a chaplain specially appointed for the task instead of being the parish priest or one of his assistants. (Such chaplains are usually members of the parochial clergy also, but what is now being discussed is their role within the schools; they do not act as parochial clergy in them.) Secondly, many religious activities and organizations which are to be found in the parish have been extended into the schools, and the children are encouraged to join them as pupils rather than as members of parishes.

The Role of the Chaplain

The close, often daily, contact with the priests of the parish, a traditional feature of parochial schools in Liverpool, is clearly not practicable in grammar schools. They draw their pupils from a wide area, often from well outside the boundaries of the city, on one hand, and of the diocese, on the other.[2] Even in the inter-parochial secondary modern school, a new phenomenon which is becoming increasingly

1. It need hardly be said that this is probably true of all grammar schools. It is argued, however, that these influences will be found in Catholic grammar schools, not that they are exclusive to them.
2. For example, one of the girls' schools included in the survey drew its pupils in 1962 from over seventy parishes. Yet this was not one of the biggest schools, nor one that was notable for serving an especially large area.

important and expedient, it has proved too difficult for the parochial clergy to look after their own children in the traditional way, and chaplains are appointed for the spiritual welfare of these pupils too. In the grammar schools, the position is even more difficult, and parochial divisions and responsibilities have even less meaning. Accordingly, the importance of the chaplain's function is correspondingly greater.

At the time when those who were interviewed were at school, the policy of appointing chaplains to all secondary schools had not been formulated. Some of the grammar schools had a chaplain by tradition, because there was a chaplain to the nuns in charge of the schools, but this was not invariably so. One of the boys' schools was run by priests, and it was a part of the custom to appoint a spiritual director to the school from amongst them. The other two boys' schools were in the hands of religious orders whose members were not priests. This meant that though they fulfilled certain duties of the chaplain, such as giving spiritual guidance, clearly they could not perform the sacramental function of a chaplain.

The tasks of the clergy which were associated with the parish in the parochial schools are completely unrelated to the parish in the grammar schools. Contact with the clergy who are not associated with one's own parish is likely to be an important factor in developing attitudes towards the priesthood. One might expect that this relationship with the chaplain would make it easier to join extra-parochial groups later on. Unfortunately, at the time those who were interviewed were at school, the role of the chaplain was less formally defined, and his status and function differed from school to school. This meant that the chaplain was, by and large, not regarded as a very important figure in the schools. It was too early to study the impact of the more precisely formulated role of the chaplain, a question which needs considering later, for it is likely to prove to be one of the most significant influences in producing attitudes towards the clergy and towards the social groups in the parish.

The uncertainty of the status and role of the chaplains at the time of the inquiry was reflected in the answers to the questions put to the former pupils. No enthusiastic remarks or explosive criticisms which sometimes greeted the mention of the parish priest in another part of the interview were made. It was plain that most were puzzled at the questions on the chaplain, and they found it difficult to remember enough to give answers. In fact, there was a considerable amount of confusion as to whether or not there actually was a chaplain in the school. Some ex-pupils remembered priests who had celebrated Mass or given Benediction, but they were uncertain whether or not they were official chaplains. The haziness of memories in this regard can perhaps be most eloquently demonstrated by the fact that contradictory information was given in all the boys' schools, and half the girls' schools. Table 8, given in numbers, not percentages, shows how divided opinions were.

TABLE 8

Chaplains as reported by the Respondents

	Reported a chaplain	Reported no chaplain
BOYS' SCHOOLS:		
1	10	5
2	1	14
3	4	8
GIRLS' SCHOOLS:		
4	11	0
5	3	11
6	1	0
7	6	2
8	3	4
9	0	1

It must be stressed that the relevant questions were not asked to find out if there were in fact chaplains at the schools, since this method would obviously have been most unreliable; direct information about chaplains was obtained from the head teachers. In the interviews with the former pupils, the aim was to discover their attitudes towards the chaplains, and above all, to see what importance they attached to them.

Memories about classes taken by the chaplains were similarly vague. Even when they were mentioned as interesting or enjoyable, the contents were forgotten by the time three years had elapsed. One girl, for instance, remembered only that the chaplain had allowed the class to knit while he talked. Those who recollected the chaplain's lessons at all (and of course not all remembered his existence) were sure of one point: that he gave lessons to the Sixth Form only, and this was confirmed by the head teachers. This implies that his influence was largely confined to the minority who completed the grammar school course.

A further probe into the relationship between chaplain and pupil asked if there were any opportunities when one could talk to the chaplain if one wished. Once again, opinions diverged. In only one school nearly all the former pupils thought that the chaplain was available in this way. It is significant that this was also the only school where they were unanimous in saying that there was a chaplain. That some believed the chaplain was available was, however, no indication that his services were used in this way. Many took the trouble to make explicit the point that neither they nor their friends had ever taken advantage of an opportunity to talk to the chaplain.

It was plain from the responses that the chaplain's role was not regarded as important. A particular priest might be singled out for praise because the pupils had liked him, but he was generally considered to be 'just the priest who came to say Mass or hold another service'.

It was interesting to discover how much the situation has changed since those who were interviewed had left school. The appointment of chaplains to all Catholic schools in the archdiocese has been accompanied by a clearer definition of their role and functions, and a growing emphasis upon their importance. There has been, too, an increasing awareness of the special problems brought about when the chaplain is given more responsibility for spiritual welfare and little means of solving the special problems which this brings about. At the moment, he does not visit the children in their homes, although it has been suggested that this would help his work.[1] If this proposal is put into practice, yet another function of the parish will be transferred to the school. This increasing stress on the importance of the chaplain will probably increase the dominance of the school community in the lives of the pupils. When they leave school, they are likely to be even less familiar with the priests of the parish than they are at present. It looks as though one of the consequences of the policy of increasing the status of the chaplain will be a further lack of interest in the parish. On the other hand, familiarity with the functions of extra-parochial clergy may make adaptations to new groupings, even the move to another parish, easier. The consequences of such policies need to be considered when they have had time to make their influence felt.

Religious Services

The appointment of the chaplain brings with it religious services in the schools. Previously there had, of course, been prayers at morning assembly, and prayers before and after lessons, which are a feature of every Catholic school. But in the parochial schools, the children are frequently taken into the parish church for Mass or Benediction,

1. V. Malone, 'Priests in School', *The Clergy Review*, N.S., XLVI (1961), 513–24.

especially on feastdays. The link between church and school is thus strengthened at every possible point. In the grammar schools, however, such services are taken by the chaplains, and are usually held in a chapel in the building, often the one belonging to the religious community responsible for running the school. Recently, too, the chaplains have been available for confession in the chapels at certain fixed times.

Another point is worth mentioning in this context. It used to be the custom in Liverpool parishes, as it still is in some other English dioceses, for there to be a children's Mass on a Sunday. This was largely identified with the parochial school children (and, of course, in many parishes, few children ever attended any other school). The receiving of one's First Communion, too, tended to be a school affair, with all the children in a class making their Communion together, and a breakfast was later held in the school. Here, then, were two ways in which the parish school children were identified with the parish, ways which excluded those who went to other schools. However, Dr. John C. Heenan has stressed the importance of the family's priority over the school on the day of the First Communion and at Sunday Mass, and both customs identifying school and parish are dying out in Liverpool.[1]

Religious Associations in the Schools

The second major way in which the grammar schools have taken over functions of the parish is through establishing within themselves religious organizations of the type normally attached to the parishes. This is presumably to encourage young Catholics to develop an understanding of the spiritual and social consequences of their beliefs within the *milieu* in which they may be living at a particular time. The hope is usually expressed that the experience of belonging to such organizations will lead not only to a deeper understanding of their faith, but will also encourage them to rejoin such groups later in life, presumably in a parochial setting. Does this in fact happen? To answer this, an attempt was made to find out if the young Catholics interviewed had belonged to such organizations, and if so, if they still belonged to them in another environment. Did they consider the experience to have been a valuable one? Was it a means for them to resume full membership of their parishes after they left school?

A variety of religious organizations and associations in the schools were remembered in the interviews. In all, nine were named, not all correctly, it may be added, even by former members of them. Only 14 per cent of the replies stated (sometimes incorrectly) that there had

1. At the time this research was being compiled Dr. Heenan was Archbishop of Liverpool. He is now Archbishop of Westminster.

been none in the schools concerned. A few complaints were made that such organizations had existed, but that no information had been made available about them.

One or two of the groups mentioned required of the members only the willingness to pray for certain intentions. Five of the organizations, however, required attendance at a weekly meeting, and the performance of a weekly task of some sort. For example, the members of the Junior Conference of the St. Vincent de Paul Society, which existed in two of the boys' schools, visited old people living near the schools. Other groups worked within the schools themselves. Only one of these five organizations was specifically designed for the pupils' needs, the Young Christian Students; the other four were junior branches of associations existing in parochial and other settings throughout the Catholic Church. A group which was reported by some of the girls was a form of the association known as the Children of Mary. This is to be distinguished from Our Lady's Sodality, included in the groups described above, because it differed in the girls' schools from the Sodality, in that the requirements of membership appeared to be vague in the extreme.

Sixty-five per cent of the replies stated that those concerned had been members of at least one of these associations at some point in their school careers, often in the Sixth Form, a point worth remembering in view of the small proportion completing the course. The former pupils of the boys' schools usually reported that membership was optional, but some of the girls believed membership was obligatory, while others thought membership was only nominally optional, a position summed up in the remark, 'Yes, you could join whichever one you wanted. I think they liked you to join one.'

Whatever the formal policy, belonging to a group was clearly taken for granted as part of the accepted way of behaviour in some schools. A protest was exceptional, although one young man did point out:

The trouble with all these things at school is that they're more or less compulsory. It's not a personal thing.

While criticisms were frequent, they were generally directed not towards the aims of the organizations but rather at what was regarded as inefficiency in the way such groups were run in the school. Sometimes, too, the school was regarded as an inadequate environment for the work the groups undertook.

In considering the views expressed towards these associations, one broad distinction can be drawn immediately. In general, the highly structured and disciplined groups, such as the St. Vincent de Paul Society and the Legion of Mary, were appreciated even by those who did not belong to them; their function could be seen and understood.[1] On the other hand, the loosely knit groups, such as the Children of Mary, were regarded as pointless. The following comments reveal how much stress was placed in the answers upon action:

I thought they were very good. They didn't shove religion to the fore. They placed emphasis on trying to help people.
It's a good thing for Catholic grammar schools to have these organizations. I thought the Legion of Mary was the best. I didn't take it particularly seriously, but I would now. You felt you were doing something good for someone.
It's a pretty good idea. You have to be that kind of person though, and I wasn't the right kind. I wasn't willing to put myself out.

Occasionally criticisms were of a personal nature. One young man, for instance, said, 'It just seemed like extra religious duties, so of course I wasn't interested.' Another remarked:

Frankly, they were not for me at the time, probably because they entailed doing things in my own time which I thought then was rather precious. Then again, the practice of religion is just not done in front of your class mates. There are basically two sides to your character, one for your class mates, one for the masters.

But many of the criticisms were made on the grounds that the less structured groups did not 'do enough'. One girl remarked on the Young Christian Students, for instance, 'I wouldn't say it did very much in school. You didn't seem to do much, just discussed things. It was more a nominal thing.' Comments on the Children of Mary were frequently scathing. Typical remarks were:

I thought it was a pretty poor do, actually. You didn't really feel as though you belonged. It was more like a lesson. Nobody liked it or tried to get you interested.
I thought it was rather peculiar. You'd better not put that down! It seemed in a way pointless.

The laconic comment of one girl sums up both the process of joining such loosely knit groups and the attitudes some developed towards them far better than an elaborate sociological description: she said, 'Everybody else did it. I just joined. That's about all.' It has already been said that the hope was sometimes expressed that the pupils would continue their membership after leaving school. In fact, there are some whose belief is more than a hope that this happens; they are convinced that it does.[2] It is all the more important, therefore, to emphasize that only 14 per cent of all those interviewed con-

1. These organizations, which were viewed with approval because of their active work, lay primary emphasis in their constitutions on the spiritual formation of members, which should then have an influence on attitudes and behaviour.
2. This statement is based on evidence collected by the interviewer while attending various meetings, both parochial and extra-parochial.

tinued their membership in any way at all, in the parish or elsewhere. A couple of young men had transferred to a parochial section of the organization to which they had belonged, and were now largely responsible for running it. A few had resumed membership on going to a Catholic Training College, but after leaving it, only a handful continued to be members, thus reducing the numbers further. Another 4 per cent said they were still members of the groups because 'Once you're a member, you're always a member'; but it was clear that no action, such as attending a meeting, had followed from this.

For the majority, then, membership ended on leaving school. Few gave a specific reason for leaving an organization. Generally the reason was simply that they had left school, as the following extracts show:

You had to make a particular effort to keep up. It was just negative. I didn't bother.
No, just because I left school. I dropped it.
It's just that most people did.
You don't continue after leaving school. I never got round to joining at church.

While one was a member of the school community, it was customary to belong, and membership was taken up easily. But on leaving school, it was dropped as readily, and for the same reason. The majority of those who belonged clearly associated membership with school life, and regarded it as something which one discontinued after leaving.[1] Thus, the optimistic proposal made in some of the schools that experience of the organizations in a school context would serve as an introduction for later membership was not borne out in the interviews. In view of the attitudes expressed, the possibility seems remote. No evidence was found which might suggest that belonging to these organizations in school made it easier to fit into the parochial community later. Only a few ex-pupils were filled with sufficient enthusiasm to continue membership after school.

Other School Activities

Another aspect of school activities is also worth mentioning, in that it shows a further way in which pupils are encouraged to live their lives within the school community. Many organizations other than the religious flourish in the schools. Apart from sports, which were particularly extensive in the boys' schools, groups were named. Some

1. These results lead to speculation as to how far this process of identifying organizations with school life may be similar to the process which is often alleged to take place in secondary modern schools, namely the identifying of church attendance or even religious beliefs with school life, practices which are abandoned after leaving.

were related to study, such as a scientific society, while others catered more for leisure time interests, such as a dramatic society or a chess club. Nearly half of those interviewed had belonged to at least one of these groups. In general they appeared to be rather fluid, and membership was on a casual basis, often embracing a whole class, but the question whether or not such activities could be classified as organizations is not particularly relevant for present purposes. What is important is the extent to which the pupils were offered opportunities to develop interests within the social structure of the school. Even when no organizations were reported, social activities of various kinds were important in this regard. Interestingly, complaints were made by those who said that there had been no organizations in their schools. Sometimes, too, others from schools where they did exist wanted more of them. It was plain that the emphasis upon the school as a source of leisure activities was generally acceptable.

The importance of the school community emerges even more clearly when patterns of friendship are considered, as they are in Chapter 10. With only one exception, all those who were interviewed had close friends in their own class. Although some had friends outside, the tendency was for friendships to be centred on the school.

Thus the dominant place of the school in the lives of most of the pupils is evident. Whether this is a deliberate policy or simply an unintended consequence of a separate policy, such an emphasis cannot fail to have its repercussions upon the attitudes and behaviour of the pupils towards other groups and activities, not only while they are at school, but later in life. No matter how desirable other activities may appear, when time is limited (it was made abundantly clear that it was), some must be neglected. Obviously, those which are considered less important will be the ones to be disregarded.

Policies of the Schools

The headteachers of the grammar schools were, it seems, often aware that their pupils might be alienated from the parish as a result of the schools' social organization and teaching. They were not unanimous in their evaluation of this, but the attitude expressed by some was that if this happened, it was a pity, but that it was largely inevitable as circumstances were at the time. The fact that there is no clear-cut policy in relation to pupils' participation in parochial activities makes the situation a delicate one. Obviously, the schools had the responsibility of getting pupils through examinations, and thus had to demand that leisure should be curtailed. On the other hand, in view of the strength of parochial loyalties in Liverpool, few would wish to impose a ban on them. Sometimes the staff mentioned to the pupils the idea of joining groups in the parish or elsewhere after leaving school, but understandably, the parish did not dominate the scene as it does in the parochial schools.[1] It would be hard to imagine how it could do so in the circumstances. The ways in which these attitudes towards the parish were communicated to pupils are described in Chapter 7.

Lest the influence of the grammar schools be seen solely as a negative one, something further must be said at this point. The view was expressed by the majority of the head teachers that it was their responsibility to develop an attachment within their pupils to their religious faith which would find its expression in the service of others. It was thought desirable that people should sometimes use organizations as a means of doing this, but that the pupils should understand that they could fulfil their apostolate without belonging to any formal groups. Religious associations are, after all, only means to an end, and while many find it helpful to belong, others prefer to remain outside. Thus, while associations and other means of developing spiritual and social responsibilities were available in the schools, and pupils were encouraged to consider joining such groups later in life, the schools concentrated on stimulating a sense of responsibility in a wider context than that of the parish. They wished the parochial organizations to be seen as one set of groupings amongst others.

In assessing the extent to which parochial loyalties have been affected as the result of grammar school education, it is worthwhile remembering that the schools have concentrated on wider responsibilities of life. It was not, as some parish priests seemed to think, that the grammar schools were careless in encouraging parochial loyalties; they saw their function as being to communicate to their pupils a sense of belonging to the Church which would find its expression in a variety of ways.

Conclusions

Here, then, is a crucial issue in the study. By emphasizing the school community, a deliberate policy has been set in motion, surrounded no doubt by activities which have grown around it and are less premeditated. What are the consequences of this policy? Were all of them intended or were some of them unplanned? It has been shown that the emphasis on the school community was an acceptable one to the pupils; most took part in activities which were not strictly related to the formal curriculum, including religious activities. But one part of the planned policy has been shown to have failed. Few continued their membership of religious associations after leaving school. Another failure was that the role of the chaplain did not strike them as important. What are the other unintended consequences of change?

1. Cf. Fichter, *Social Relations, op. cit.*, p. 175.

What effect has this stress upon the school had upon their attitudes towards other groups within the Church—the parish, for instance? It is with these questions that the following chapters are concerned. The school does not exist in a vacuum, and when a complex network of social relationships, groups and beliefs are established around it, these are bound to develop attitudes and ways of behaving which will have repercussions for pupils in later life, not only as individuals, but also as members of the community as a whole.

Chapter 6

THE ROLE OF THE PRIEST

IN considering the reaction of former pupils of grammar schools to the social groupings of the Roman Catholic Church, the first point of departure is necessarily that of the parish. It is because of the central importance of the priesthood in the parish that this analysis begins with the relationship between clergy and laity. The confrontation of tradition with rapid social change is seen in this relationship perhaps more clearly than in any other way. The relationship between pastor and parishioner in Liverpool is one which has grown in such a manner that it has been very strictly governed by tradition. It involves certain clearly defined attitudes and patterns of behaviour on both sides. What, then, has happened when changes are brought about in the social *milieu* in which this elaborate role system between priest and people has developed? Will the old relationship be possible in these circumstances, or will a new one develop? How do priests and their new parishioners see one another in this context?

The Traditional Role of the Priest

Before describing the findings of this study, it is essential to describe the traditional roles of priest and parishioners and the social context in which they developed. In this way, it should be possible to show what are the factors which are operating as agents of change, and in which directions these changes lie. When reference was made in the first chapter to the traditional grouping of Liverpool Catholics around the parish, particular attention was drawn to the dominant role of the priesthood in the parochial system. This is a feature of the parochial structure in general. One of the most important writers on the sociological aspects of the parish comments:

The priest is the key person in any Catholic parish, and his role in the functioning of the parochial system is so important that without him the parish would cease to exist. All parochial activities strictly so-called, directly or indirectly, depend on the priest. They touch on him in some way even when they do not completely revolve around him.[1]

Historically, the position of the priesthood has been a factor of tremendous importance in the development of Catholicism in Liver-

---

1. J. H. Fichter, *Social Relations, op. cit.*, p. 123. Cf. L. Neundorfer, 'Office and Service. The Function of the Church in modern society', *Social Compass*, VII, 4 (1960); see especially p. 289 on the function of the priest in the parish.

pool. It is clear that the parish priest was not merely a leader in the religious sphere but also in the social life of Catholics in general.[1] The way in which this relationship has persisted in the south end dock area of Liverpool to the present time is described by Mays:

One cannot help . . . being impressed by the close identification of priests, teachers and parishioners, compared with which the activities of some of the other churches in the district fade into insignificance. The great strength of the Roman Catholic priesthood lies in their amazing ability to share their parishioners' life while, at the same time, maintaining a spiritual aloofness which adds compelling force to their leadership . . . The Parish Priest dominates the neighbourhood. He is everyone's moral mentor. He keeps a firm hold on the schools and is the final arbiter in all disputes.[2]

Similarly, in describing the results of interviews carried out in a Liverpool parish, Ward comments that the answers not only reflected the central position of the priest in the parish, but that it was clear there was a 'close relationship and continual involvement of priest and people'.[3] Evidence collected in the course of the present survey amply confirmed these findings, and revealed the depth of the identification of interests.

The deep respect of the faithful for the clergy has long been regarded as a characteristic feature of Catholicism in Liverpool. This attitude has developed in such a way that the priest has come to be considered as an authority in matters which are not directly related to the sphere of religion. One of the priests interviewed in the present study remarked:

Here in Liverpool there is a remarkable loyalty and respect for the priesthood. It's to be found here more than anywhere else. In fact, people often pay the respect to the man which is due to the priesthood.[4]

The ways in which the attitude of respect towards the priesthood has been carried over into other areas of behaviour can be seen in the description of what was expected in St. Catherine's parish of 'the priest' (for often his personal identity is absorbed in his role):

The priest . . . was reported to have been asked for advice on the most varied subjects . . . In most of these other spheres, the role of the priest appeared to be primarily that of a person who was interested and would listen to the story and talk about the problem although his contribution

1. T. Burke, op. cit., and M. McNarney, 'La Vie Paroissiale', in Catholicisme Anglais, Paris, 1958.
2. Op. cit., p. 58.
3. Op. cit., p. 63.
4. A similar point is made by J. J. Kane, Catholic-Protestant Conflicts in America, Chicago, 1955, p. 53. For discussion of the distinction between the priest and the priesthood, see Pope Pius XI, Ad Catholici Sacerdoti, 1935, second edition of English translation, London, 1955, and Pope Pius XII, Mediator Dei, London, 1959; see also Pastoral Letters of Cardinal Suhard, London, 1955.

might be more related to supernatural truths than to a practical solution of the difficulty.[1]

The present study, too, confirmed how the priest was expected by many of his parishioners to cope with all sorts of situations. As one parish priest remarked in the course of an interview, indicating a pile of requests for references for jobs, 'It seems that no-one can get a job peeling potatoes in the Adelphi [hotel] without a reference from me!'

The way in which shared adversity drew priests and parishioners together has already been pointed out. Upon the basis of such experiences, a whole social system has developed to foster the close relationship. For instance, stress has customarily been laid in Liverpool upon the visitation of parishioners' homes by the clergy, and Ward has shown how vital a factor this is in maintaining the bond between the two.[2]

Another point of contact which is of crucial importance in establishing and maintaining this relationship is the parish school, a characteristic feature of the parochial system.[3] The importance of the school in fostering parochial loyalties in various ways has often been pointed out,[4] but what is particularly relevant for the present purposes is the role it plays in establishing and developing the relationship between priests and parishioners. The very struggle to build and maintain these schools is clearly a means of fostering a sense of shared concern and responsibility. Moreover, in parochial schools in Liverpool, the children are accustomed to seeing the priests frequently, often each day in some schools. Thus, the priest becomes a familiar figure in their lives and they learn what sort of behaviour is expected of them in relation to him. The priests, in turn, are able, through these visits, to get to know their children intimately.

The question is now asked, can this relationship between priest and parishioner, developing as it has in a particular social context, remain unchanged when some of the young parishioners leave the parochial school at the age of eleven to attend grammar schools? If this intimate contact is lacking at school, what sort of a relationship will grow up later? It was suggested as a hypothesis to be tested in this research that the relationship between the parochial clergy and parishioners who went to grammar schools would be characterized by a lack of familiarity on both sides; and that this would lead at

1. Ward, op. cit., pp. 62–3.
2. The tradition of visitation of the homes by the clergy is now formalized in the Synodal Regulations. Liverpool Archdiocesan Synod XXIV, 1955. See C. K. Ward, 'Priests and People: A Study of Parish Visitation in an English City', Sociologia Religiosa, V, 7 (1961), 79–84.
3. Cf. W. Lloyd Warner and L. Srole, op. cit., p. 236.
4. Cf. Fichter, op. cit., and Ward, op. cit., p. 94.

times to mutual confusion as to the behaviour which was expected of them.[1] The complementary studies of the attitudes of parishioners and clergy are now presented to show how each group sees the other and what they expect of one another.

The Attitudes of the Grammar School Parishioners

As a preliminary step to discovering the nature of the relationship between the clergy and the grammar school parishioners, the extent to which the latter acknowledged the central position of the priest in the parish is discussed. The recognition—or failure to give recognition—of this status is an indication of how the most important aspect of the priest's role was accepted or rejected by these young parishioners.

The way in which the position of the clergy in the parish was acknowledged emerges plainly from this study. In fact, although this finding was expected, the extent to which it was apparent in the interviews came as a surprise to the investigator. It must be emphasized that those who were interviewed were not asked questions at any point about the clergy, other than how often they saw them. What was remarkable was the degree to which references were made to them throughout this section of the interview. The fact, then, that these comments were made spontaneously makes them all the more significant and valuable.

The way in which the priest is associated with the ultimate responsibility for what happens in the parish was particularly apparent when respondents were attempting to tell the interviewer who organized parochial activities. Thirty-one per cent had no knowledge of parochial activities but answered this question. Nearly all of them suggested that the priest was the chief organizer. Answers typical of this group of replies were:

I don't know. I think the parish priest from what I can make out.
Apart from the parish priest being at the head, I couldn't say.
I don't know really. I presume the clergy.

Out of another 32 per cent whose subsequent answers indicated some knowledge of parochial activities, over half mentioned the clergy as being responsible for running parochial affairs. As one of them put it, 'The parish priest—literally!'

When the way in which their parishes were organized was mentioned, 36 per cent spontaneously referred in their replies to the clergy, although there was nothing in the question to suggest this answer. The percentage is all the more noticeable when one con-

1. Cf. L. Egberink, 'La Paroisse—quelques aspects des recherches', *Social Compass*, VI, 2 (1958), p. 64.

siders that a large proportion of the group had little knowledge of parish activities and even less interest, and tended consequently to give cautious answers to such questions. Almost half of these people who mentioned the clergy answered in terms of the personalities of individual priests. Some of these replies were favourable, as the following examples show:

I think it's pretty good. The old parish priest here is very enthusiastic. He does a lot for the church and visits a good deal.

Administratively, this parish is one of the most progressive. That's through the work of the parish priest.

Everyone thinks the world of the parish priest.

Some, on the other hand, were critical of individual priests, and voiced their opinions in no uncertain way; examples were:

I've a very poor opinion of it. The parish priest is a bit of a stick in the mud with regard to activities. In general, it's not very well organized. A new parish priest would be a good thing here.

I think about organization from the parish priest's point of view—the parish is very well organized. You can't move for priests. I've never seen more money conscious priests in my life.

The remainder of this 36 per cent referred to the clergy in a more general context. A student, who had attended a private school before the age of eleven, replied, for instance:

I've never come up against it. The priest sees us at church and knows we were at Catholic schools. He never makes much bother about us.

The matter of the priest's visits was mentioned frequently in answering this question. Some, it is important to note, even appeared to identify the organization of the parish with this visitation. An example of this approach can be found in the appreciative comment of a young teacher:

It's pretty good. It's been brought to a fine art over the years. If you never go to church even, the priest comes every three weeks. If you were *ever* a Catholic!

It was plain that many shared the views of St. Catherine's parishioners on the importance of the priest's visits.[1] Where these visits were reported to be rare, this was lamented. People clearly had an ideal in mind in this context, and related behaviour to that concept. A significant remark was, 'There should be greater contact between the clergy and people of the parish.' Unlike the parishioners in Ward's study, many answers showed resentment at the practice in some parishes of the priest collecting money for parochial funds during his visit. Even when those who complained said they realized the

1. Ward, *op. cit.*, p. 61.

pressures of school projects and other commitments were strong, they evidently regarded this aspect of the priest's role as distasteful, in that it associated him with the collection of money. The terse comment, 'You don't see the priest unless he wants money', summed up this attitude.

Spontaneous references to the priest were also made when those who had lived in other parishes expressed preference for one of these parishes. It was interesting to see that occasionally a person who had lived in a central Liverpool parish, or in another parish where contact with the clergy was proverbial, missed this relationship on moving to the suburbs. The following replies indicate how strange the new relationship might seem:

This is a queer parish. We used to see more of the priests in the other parish. You knew them better, saw them more. They were a part of your life. Here you just go to Mass.

There's a great contrast in this parish and the one where I used to live in the centre. You had frequent visits from the priests. There's a lot of contact with the priest there.

The importance of the priest's personality was revealed by a young man when he stated his preference for the parish in which he had previously lived:

The other one. The parish priest was really down to earth. He's dead better than the one up the road. I'm not meaning any ill-will, but he's existing in a cloud. He comes to meet people, but he can't come to grips. I think the character of the parish priest has a great effect on the parish. It's enormous.

Similarly, in discussing what activities should be provided in the ideal parish, answers often reflected the central importance of the priest. One person summed up this feeling by saying at the end of his reply, 'It all boils down to the parish priest.' Clearly, then, those who were interviewed were well aware of the dominant role of the priest in the parochial system. But what of the 'close relationship and continual involvement of priests and people' which was a characteristic feature of St. Catherine's parish? How far was such a situation true of those who had been to grammar schools?

Contact with the Parochial Clergy

In considering the contact which those who were interviewed had at an early age with their parish priests, it is important to remember that half of the boys and just under half of the girls had attended their own parochial schools before going to grammar schools. This was particularly useful for the purposes of analysis, in that their contact with the priest in the past can be compared with the contact of those who did not attend their parish schools. There were a few more who subsequently went to private schools before going to grammar schools who had also attended their parish schools for a short time. But it must be stressed that approximately half of those who were interviewed had never experienced the close contact with the priests which exists in the parochial school. Even those who had attended the parochial schools had, of course, only done so until about the age of eleven.

Those who had attended the parish schools at some point had clear recollections of the priests 'popping in and out'. Comments such as, 'The church was on the doorstep', emphasized the relationship between the geographical and social proximity of school and church. This association between church and school was strengthened, too, by the way in which they were frequently taken into the church for services. After leaving the parochial schools, a great difference in contact resulted. They reported that after going to grammar schools they had seen little of the priests, apart from visits to their homes. The comment of a young man who was interviewed in the early stages of the fieldwork gives some indication of the frame of mind of such a person: 'After I left the parish school, the priest was just the person who said Mass on Sundays.'

Present contact with the parochial clergy varied enormously. Eight per cent, for instance, said they never saw the priests from their parishes at all, while another eight per cent said the only time they saw the priests was at church or in the street. Sixty per cent reported that their only contact with the priests was when the latter visited their homes. The reported frequency of the visits varied enormously, from, at one end of the scale, once a month or even more often, as 35 per cent reported, to, at the other end, 20 per cent who reported that the visits were rare. Six per cent claimed, reporting the frequency of the priests' visits to the homes of the parish, that their own families were not visited.

It is important to bear two points in mind in considering these answers. Firstly, account was taken of the frequency of visitation reported by respondents, not that reported by parish priests, because the interviewer wanted to discover the frequency of the visits as perceived by those who were interviewed. Secondly, this information does not necessarily indicate how often those who were interviewed actually saw the priests for another reason; they sometimes added that they were usually out when the priest called. Some of those who were interviewed were studying away from home for part of the year, and so missed the visits.

Those who were engaged in parochial activities, or whose families were active in the parish, saw the priests far more often than the others. Twenty-three per cent reported seeing the priests either at parochial meetings of one sort or another, or when the priests called at their homes on extra visits to discuss matters relating to the parish activities in which they or others of the family took part. As one person from a family which was active in parochial affairs explained, 'Officially, they come once a quarter, but with us being involved, they're always coming.'

Thus, the present contact of these parishioners with the parochial clergy varied a great deal. Many were clearly unfamiliar with their parish priests and saw little of them. On the other hand, the answers of those who frequently saw the priests reflected far more acceptance of the different aspects of the priest's role than the replies of those who reported seeing them rarely. As one would expect, the visitation of the homes seemed to be a crucial factor in producing and maintaining this understanding. In the present circumstances where contact in the schools has been lacking, it is probably all the more important.

How, then, did these young people view the role of the priest? How far was the old role which he had assumed in earlier generations acceptable to them? What did they expect of him?

Opinions on the Role of the Priest

It seems that, unlike previous generations of Catholics, these young people distinguished between the priesthood and the individual priest. While they respected the former, they were sometimes highly critical of individual priests. But this dislike or annoyance did not lead to generalizations about all priests. They did not confuse the sacramental dignity with personal faults. It is significant, for example, that only one person in discussing reasons why Catholics stopped going to church suggested that this was because of a quarrel with the priest, instancing his own father. It was noticeable, too, that in none of the interviews was there any trace of real anti-clericalism of the sort which is sometimes found abroad.

However, certain aspects of the priest's role in the parish were rejected. The dislike of the priest collecting money has already been mentioned. But perhaps the most significant rejection discovered in the course of the survey lies in the rebellion expressed in some answers at the extent to which the parish priest controls all parochial affairs. It is probable that those who gave such answers did not object to his ultimate control, but they were unable to understand why he should be responsible for the day to day running of parochial activities. This was summed up in the remark, 'Far too much of the parish work which should be done by lay people and many jobs which a lay person could do are done by the priest.'

It was plain, too, that they did not look to him for advice in matters not directly related to the spiritual sphere, like many other Catholics. Even in the realm of doctrine and moral questions, there were criticisms at times of the alleged ignorance of some priests. Most of all, they objected to an attitude which they believed existed in the minds of some of the parochial clergy; their feelings are probably best summed up by an American writer on a similar situation:

. . . it has been suggested that large numbers of the clergy half-unconsciously conceive the laity as a kind of spiritual proletariat. They expect little from them in terms of mature Christian knowledge, and in terms of Christian living often not much more than that they will 'obey the rules'.[1]

Many who were interviewed felt similarly, and thought that the parochial clergy did not expect sufficient from them in the way of understanding the Church's teaching. What was particularly significant was that the resentment felt over this point was especially strong among university students interviewed in the course of the research. While the general body of Catholic students might not have made much effort to study their faith in depth, there were amongst them some, especially older students and graduates, who had applied themselves to theology and philosophy over a period of years. Such people were often distressed or angered at the attitude their parish priests sometimes took towards their knowledge. It might be added that even at Sixth Form level there is clearly a growing nucleus of young people who, after studying the Church's liturgy in school, find it difficult to understand why the parochial clergy may be reluctant to introduce such changes as the Dialogue Mass. While such people may still be in the minority, the writer was impressed at several conferences attended during the fieldwork to discover how passionately some of these pupils felt about such topics. Evidently their views could only alienate them to some degree from more conservative members of the clergy.

Such conferences introduce a feature which seems to be of fundamental importance in developing attitudes towards the clergy. With the increasing numbers of courses and conferences designed for those who are still at school, more and more young Catholics from grammar schools are coming into contact with extra-parochial clergy, especially members of religious orders and congregations, whose education and experiences tend to be very different from those of the secular clergy working in the parishes. As one would expect, the priests selected to give talks at such meetings are usually lively and stimulating speakers. Unlike the parish priest giving his sermon to a congregation of all ages and levels of education, and responsible in Canon Law for the care of all these people entrusted to him, a

1. T. F. O'Dea, *American Catholic Dilemma. An Inquiry into the Intellectual Life*, New York, 1958.

speaker at such a meeting has a more specialized task. Designed historically as 'shock troops', the members of religious orders outside the parochial structure have a function very different from that of the parochial clergy. Towards young people whose critical faculty has probably already been encouraged at school, the priest at a conference can display an attitude totally different from that which would be appropriate for the parish priest with his heavy pastoral responsibility. At a comparatively early age, the young Catholic may not appreciate the differences in responsibility and function which exist between the clergy, and may find the views of extra-parochial clergy much more attractive than those he finds in the parish. As a result, his attitude towards his own pastor may become increasingly intolerant because of the ideas he has learned from clergy outside the parish. At university or college, this contact with the extra-parochial clergy is likely to increase, and the student may grow accustomed to ways of thinking and reacting in the religious sphere which are fundamentally different from those of his parish priest.

The Attitudes of the Parish Priests

To complete the analysis of the relationship between the parochial clergy and Catholics who had been to grammar schools, interviews were carried out with some parish priests. It is remarkable that while several studies have been carried out in different countries on the attitudes of various sections of the laity towards the priest,[1] little attention has been given as yet to the systematic study of the ways in which the Catholic clergy view the faithful—an interesting omission in view of the fact that a very high proportion of those currently engaged in socio-religious research are themselves members of the clergy. Even in such an investigation as this, which was essentially exploratory, it was considered important to complement the study of the attitudes of the former pupils of grammar schools with an inquiry into the views of some of the clergy. Only tentative suggestions can

1. See, for instance, J. M. Jammes, 'Les Catholiques Américains et le Sacerdoce', *Chronique Sociale de France*, I, 63ᵉ année (1955), 23–36; F. Boulard, 'Comment les Chrétiens de France voient le Prêtre', in *Etudes sur le Sacrement de l'Ordre*, Paris, 1957; P. Rabin, 'What youths think of the priest and the religious life', *Lumen Vitae*, VIII, 4 (1953), 667–81; A. Gemelli, 'Quello che i lavorati pensano di noi sacerdoti', *Rivista del Clero Italiano*, 23 (1942), 305–9. The writer was unable to trace any studies dealing with the systematic collection of the opinions and attitudes of Roman Catholic priests, although some surveys include interviews with members of the clergy. There are, on the other hand, several studies which consider the views of Protestant ministers, notably J. Highet, *The Scottish Churches*, London, 1960. Highet tried to include in this survey of the religious situation in Scotland the views of Roman Catholic clergy, but the response was disappointing; as the author points out, this was not altogether surprising since 'neither archbishop nor priest could be expected to enthuse much over a project related (even if unofficially) to the Fourth Centenary of the Reformation', p. 209.

be made at this stage, but it is plain that such inquiries into clerical attitudes would be very illuminating in the investigation of religious systems.

In the early stages of the fieldwork, it was put to the investigator that any efforts to collect information and opinions from the clergy would be frustrated, because they would be unwilling to co-operate in the inquiry. Nevertheless, it was decided to approach them. A random sample was considered impracticable, so all the parish priests from the seven parishes to each of which four or more of the former pupils interviewed belonged were approached. Other parishes were selected for various reasons. A few were chosen because only a handful of children living there attended grammar schools and it was important to obtain comparisons; others on the grounds that they were commonly believed to be 'traditional' parishes, and finally two on new housing estates. In all, information was collected from priests in sixteen parishes in the city of Liverpool. In several other parishes, information was either given or attempts were made to obtain it, but as what was obtained was not of any great value, it has not been used in the study. In not one case was the interviewer refused information. Although a few pastors were clearly amused at the idea of the in- quiry, most were extremely helpful, and some went to considerable trouble to amplify their statements, wherever possible, by making records of various kinds available. Verbatim extracts from these interviews are quoted at some length because they reveal the manner in which the priests concerned saw the situation in a way which could never be adequately described by paraphrase or analysis.

Although it cannot be said that there was unanimity in the replies, certain trends were nevertheless apparent. It was immediately plain that for most of the parish priests interviewed, the question of gram- mar school education was a live issue. When children left the parochial schools to go to grammar schools, some evidently saw this as the removal of these children from their care, and were con- cerned. Their comments revealed how strongly some felt about this. One of them said simply, 'There's no doubt it's a great grief to a parish priest to lose his children in this way.' Another, pastor of a large parish from which a high proportion of children went to gram- mar schools, expressed similar sentiments:

We feel they are no longer children of the parish. The priests have no con- trol over them. We are fathers to them in the parish school . . . It's the same [as the grammar schools] in all these secondary modern schools which are combined in parishes . . . The children have that idea, too. We have no control over them.

It was evident that most saw grammar school pupils as a different section from their other parishioners, one which often created special

problems, and as people whose views were hard to understand. Most
of the priests agreed that when the children started attending grammar
schools their manner changed towards the priests. A priest in a working class area commented, 'The kids here shout, "Hello, Father,"
grab you and run round you,' adding, 'The grammar school type
won't do that.' Some expressed bewilderment at this change in attitude, which in its extreme form was reported as lack of respect for the
authority of the priest. For instance, in a suburban parish, the pastor
had this to say of his grammar school children:

They change completely unless their homes are good. They think they have
learned a lot. They overlook the fact that they are only beginning to learn.
We notice it with the altar boys in the sacristy right away . . . They seem to
think they're in a position to answer you back.

Another parish priest in the suburbs commented, 'They lose their
respect for authority, and their diligence in joining in activities proposed by their parish priest.' The experiences of one pastor illustrate
the difference of outlook between them. This priest had felt for some
time that those who had been to grammar schools were in a position
to be much more active in the parish. Accordingly, speaking from the
pulpit one Sunday morning, he had requested his parishioners of all
ages who had been to grammar schools to come to see him after
Mass. Few responded to the invitation. After requests had been made
on four successive Sundays, the majority eventually came. On inquiry, he discovered that they had been reluctant to come until they
knew what he wanted. For him, it was enough that he as their pastor
had asked them to come, and he commented on their behaviour,
'This is not *my* interpretation of respectful obedience.'

A point raised by three parish priests was the reluctance of grammar school boys to acknowledge them in the street. 'You find that
the parish school boys always do that', said one. Another, who had
remarked on this spontaneously, told the interviewer this was not a
new phenomenon: he had been astonished as far back as twenty
years ago at this failure on the part of boys at grammar schools to
greet the priest. The boys' schools were strongly criticized for allow-
ing this to happen.

Complaints about lack of respect for the priest's authority came
from all the parishes where there was a noticeable proportion of middle class parishioners, with one exception; it is perhaps worth noting
that the pastor of that parish had received an education which was
vastly different from the type most of the parochial clergy had known.
It is important, however, that not all were agreed that the change of
manner on the part of grammar school children was a matter for
either concern or regret. One point of view was expressed by the
priest who said:

There is a change in their attitude towards the priest. The parochial school children know him and run round him. The grammar school children haven't the same familiarity. The relationship changes. I think it's just as well. They have a different view of the priest. I don't think they lose their respect in the Catholic sense. They're more shy with the priest. There's not the same contact. They don't want to be babyish.

Another priest, who saw matters in much the same light, spoke of an area in which he had worked, a region where respect for the priest is regarded as particularly strong:

It's 'Hello, Father', and everything . . . If anyone said anything to you, their fists would be up in 'Catholic Action'. They're very respectful—but they won't go to church.

He then went on to compare this with the attitude of parishioners in a suburban parish where he had once been a curate. He found them much more reserved in their manner towards him, and slower to accept him, but he regarded them as 'the finest Catholics you'd find'.

Aware of the criticisms made by fellow priests that grammar school parishioners lacked respect, another priest commented:

It depends on what's at the back of it. If you could say that by passing the priest in the street, they didn't want to acknowledge the priest as such, there'd be something in it. But that's very doubtful. If you're going to have a Catholic community, the priest has to be taken for granted.

However they evaluated the change in the relationship with this emerging section, it was plain that the parish priests saw their grammar school pupils as different from other parishioners, and some found their behaviour puzzling, and at times annoying.

Conclusions

It has been said of the relationship between priest and parishioner that 'Both the formal definitions of Canon Law as well as tradition have so completely conditioned them to this relationship that it is taken for granted as a commonplace.'[1] But this study of the opinions and attitudes of priests and parishioners reveals that if a social system is altered structurally, the interaction between groups within it is also affected, and this applies to the relationship between priest and grammar school pupil. Lack of familiarity between priest and grammar school parishioner is making it difficult for each to understand what the other expects of him. No longer are both as clearly aware as they used to be of the rights and obligations which they are required to respect and discharge towards one another. The priest sees these parishioners as lost from his care, while the parishioner is unable to understand how to pay his respects to the priest. He is not

1. J. D. Donovan, 'The Social Structure of the Parish', in Nuesse and Harte, *op. cit.*, p. 83.

prepared to give the obedience which the pastor demands, while the priest does not ask of him the sort of service that he is willing to give. On the one hand, the priest is not accustomed to lay initiative, and does not tend to welcome it. On the other, the traditional attitudes surrounding the relationship have been disturbed on the side of the laity by a new form of education. This emerging section of Catholics going to grammar schools has, indeed, not been educated in the traditional context, but is expected to fit into it afterwards. It was obvious that lack of familiarity has led on some occasions to confused relationships between priests and parishioners, and that this confusion may even amount at times to conflict.

Educational change has altered the social status of some of the young parishioners, and in so doing has disturbed the balance of the relationship between priest and parishioner. The situation is a difficult one. There are some who would describe the parish priests' attitude as authoritarian and outdated. Others might see the grammar school parishioners as thoughtless and disrespectful. It was not the aim of this inquiry to assess the degree of justification of one side or the other, but rather to show how changing institutions affect attitudes and behaviour. What is appropriate to one situation may be disfunctional in other circumstances, and it must be borne in mind that the numerous roles which were assigned to the priest by earlier generations, for the most part poor and badly educated, cannot but be less acceptable in the changing circumstances of today.

As a result, tension has developed. Conflicting policies have been introduced, some formally, others by implication, and they have left both priest and parishioner bewildered. The education of the clergy apart from the laity may make it difficult at times for each to communicate with the other. The young Catholic is encouraged at his grammar school to develop loyalties to the school and he has little time for parochial activities; he sees little of his parish priest. He is not taught, through the informal processes of learning as well as by precept, how he should behave towards his parish priest. So, when he leaves school he is unsure of what is expected of him; he is aware only of certain aspects of his role and that of the priest which he does not like. At school, college, or university, he meets the extra-parochial clergy, but they do not help him to adjust to the relationship with his parish priest. In fact, by their criticisms of the conservative approach of the parochial clergy, they may make the process even more difficult, as has already been pointed out.

The priest, on the other hand, feels he has 'lost' his children when they go to grammar schools. There they learn attitudes towards Catholicism which are unfamiliar to him, and so the behaviour of such people may become an enigma to him. They are still his parishioners, he is still responsible for their spiritual care, yet they often do not want even this from him, preferring to go elsewhere, a point which the next chapter discusses.

The tension arises not as a result of individual disharmony, or disagreement, but as a consequence of the changing social system which sometimes leads to confusion in loyalties over religious institutions and responsibilities. The transformation of the social structure of Catholicism in Liverpool calls for the development of a new relationship between clergy and laity. The growing importance of the theology of the laity in the Church is a promising indication of what may be achieved in the future. Perhaps, too, the elimination of some of the auxiliary roles of the pastor, which may often be unrelated to the priesthood, may result ultimately in a deeper appreciation of the sacramental functions of the clergy.

Chapter 7

THE PARISH

In describing the attitudes of ex-grammar school pupils to the parochial clergy, the central figure in each parish, attitudes towards the parish itself have already been implied in the argument. This chapter shows in greater detail how these young Catholics regarded the parish, and what part they took in its activities. The extent to which it has been, and still is for many Catholics, an important focus of social life in the city has been emphasized already. Unlike the situation in many other countries, the idea of the parish as a social community seems still to be important.[1] How far the present generation see it as important to their lives is another matter, and this will be dealt with later. The results of the detailed investigation amongst the former pupils of grammar schools must first be described.

Attention has been drawn in Chapter 5 to the great stress laid in Catholic grammar school education upon the school, as opposed to the parish. How far, then, has this resulted in the latter being regarded as comparatively unimportant by the former pupils? Do they have any sense of belonging to it, and if so, what impact does this make on their lives? Participation in activities is probably the most obvious indication of a person's involvement in the parish. The extent to which the investigation showed that this actually took place will, therefore, be described. But, as it has been argued in Chapter 2, behaviour needs to be studied in the light of attitudes; accordingly, both must be considered.

Participation in Parochial Activities

It has already been said that the ex-pupils' homes were scattered throughout the city. In all, as many as thirty-nine parishes in the archdiocese of Liverpool were represented in the survey, and four or more young people came from each of seven of these. Forty per cent had lived in their present parishes all their lives. All knew to which parish they belonged, but several said spontaneously that they never attended their own churches. Their preference for other churches was not altogether surprising in view of the way in which the paro-

---

1. Some very interesting and stimulating observations on contemporary ideas and practices in the parish, especially with regard to its organic life, are made in J. Foster, *Requiem for a Parish*, Westminster, Maryland, 1962. See also J. Fitzsimons, 'The Life of the Parish', *Worship*, N.S., XXVI, 6 (1952), 304–10.

chial boundaries are drawn. More than one person lived nearer to another parish church than to his own, while others preferred to attend a local convent or monastery.

Twelve per cent said immediately that they had no knowledge of the activities which existed in their parishes. The majority could, however, name some if not all of the existing societies concerned; some were named inaccurately. Many had obtained their information from the notices which are read out in church on Sundays, and it was soon evident that a considerable number knew no more than the names of the societies.

The impact a social institution may make on a person's life can take a variety of forms; but participation in its activities is usually a straightforward indication that the individual is either interested, or feels a sense of obligation to take some hand in its affairs.[1] To include all possible activities, no distinction was drawn in the fieldwork about type of participation or frequency. Every activity was included, even attendance at occasional functions such as garden parties.

On being asked about participation in parochial activities, as many as 81 per cent said immediately that they took no part at all in them. Thus, only 19 per cent took part in some form of activities related to the parish. The extent to which these people were involved varied enormously. Participation included serving on the altar or singing in the choir on Sundays, and taking an active role in several groups simultaneously. On the other hand, a young man confined his activities to helping in the collection of money for parochial funds through the football pools' system; others who helped in fund-raising activities were also active in other ways. A couple of young men were active members of the St. Vincent de Paul Society in their parish. For 6 per cent, the main interest of the groups to which they belonged was social; at the meetings they could keep in touch with friends. Sometimes, however, these groups demanded the acceptance of spiritual obligations, but the stringency with which these were observed varied. For instance, a young man, who was an agnostic, unknown to his family, attended the men's club, but had not fulfilled the requirement of monthly Communion, and had not done so for some time.[2]

Eleven per cent were involved in a number of activities simultaneously. Clearly what Ward says of St. Catherine's active parish-

1. Pin makes the point that willingness to take part in the social life of the parish cannot be equated with spiritual fervour. *Op. cit.*, p. 237. In the present study, for example, a young man who was an agnostic was a member of a parish society.
2. Two young men reported that they had left the men's club because of this obligation; they went to Communion regularly, but objected to the rule, which they thought savoured of 'compulsory religion'.

ioners could be said of them: 'The process was cumulative; "one thing leads to another" was a common phrase in the interviews.'[1] Recruitment, too, was similar to that which obtained in St. Catherine's parish. The usual ways of joining groups were through the family, friends, or at the request of one of the priests. It was rare, it seems, for someone to take the initiative himself when it came to joining parish organizations.

For only 19 per cent of these young parishioners, then, membership of the parish resulted in taking part in parish activities; in the case of 11 per cent this meant multiple involvement. At the other end of the scale, the same proportion did not feel any sense of obligation to attend the parish church: 11 per cent said that they often went to other churches; as one of them put it, 'I go to Mass there sometimes —but there are others just as near.'[2]

There are several churches which cater for the needs of those who choose to stay away from their own parishes. A monastery church in one of the suburbs, for instance, attracts people from several parishes, not only because of its convenience but also for the sake of its atmosphere and its manner of conducting services.[3] To many who have been to grammar schools, a factor of importance in selecting a church is to be found in their appreciation of the dignity and relevance of the Church's liturgy; as a result of their experiences in school, they are often critical of more conservative attitudes in their own parishes. Other churches on the bus routes draw their congregations from a wide area. Several churches in the city centre offer lunchtime Masses, and attract many people to these day by day. One of these parishes caters for the needs of city workers not only in this way, but also through organizing an association which enables them to meet socially. For many, contact with fellow workers is now more important than social relationships in the home parish. The growing prevalence of daily evening and midday Masses is also leading more people to seek a convenient Mass; this often means attending a church outside one's own parish. The Cathedral Crypt, too, draws others to it. Urban living of itself is thus, it seems, lessening the importance of parochial ties.

While participation in activities is a useful indication of interest in the parish, it is not decisive for present purposes. Those who were interviewed included a high proportion who had only just completed or were in the final stage of their training. It could be said, therefore, and it often is, that it is lack of time which prevents at least some of

1. *Op. cit.*, p. 71.
2. Cf. Ward, *op. cit.*, pp. 44–5.
3. Since the fieldwork was carried out, this church has been given the status of a parish.

them from taking a wider part in parish activities. If this argument is taken to its ultimate conclusion, it might be expected that such people would be willing to join parochial associations later in life. It seemed, however, far more likely that it was lack of interest rather than lack of time which lay at the root of the matter. The attitudes towards the parish expressed by those who were interviewed are, therefore, considered in detail to test this theory.

Attitudes Towards the Parish

As soon as the topic of the parish was introduced, it was immediately plain that many of those interviewed regarded the parish with little interest; their comments revealed vividly that the parish was an irrelevance in their lives. As many as 40 per cent were prepared to say from the outset that they did not know enough about parochial activities to offer an opinion. Replies such as, 'Actually, I've no personal experience of them', and 'I don't know. I don't bother much about them', were typical. It was interesting to see how often the idea, 'I've never thought about them', was echoed in the replies.

Thirty-three per cent gave views on parochial activities which could be classified as favourable, but this statement must be qualified. Only a few spoke as enthusiastically as the young man who said, 'They're a good thing. An essential part of the community and of Catholic life.' Most of the favourable answers indicated that parochial activities were considered to be 'a good thing'—for other people. Such attitudes can best be described as tolerant. Some favourable remarks stressed the ways in which others' needs, but not one's own, were met through the parish:

Well, they're very good in the parish for people. A lot go and find something to interest them. They don't really cater for my interests. There was no youth club when I was younger, and I found interests elsewhere.

It's all right for people who enjoy them. They're essential to the parish. Good things, definitely.

Occasionally, answers revealed why it was that some people regarded themselves as different from those who took part in parish activities. In answers to these and subsequent questions, it could be seen that formally organized activities of any kind were often unpopular. One young man summed up these ideas thus:

They're all right. All these activities are all right if you like to be in a group. I don't like any of them for myself. I don't like people set in authority in my leisure time. It's all right at work.

Probably, too, some of the members of working class parishes found they had little in common with their fellows. But it was noticeable that, perhaps out of awkwardness or perhaps because it was obvious, few referred explicitly to social class. A university student remarked, 'The type of people who go are so different, I don't think I'd mix in at all.' Another said with considerable embarrassment:

They're excellent organizations in a working class area. But—I'm going to prove myself the biggest snob in the world—which I am—I'd stick out like a sore thumb.

Unfavourable comments on parochial activities were made by 20 per cent. Some of these were general in tone. For instance, one person said vehemently, 'They're worse than useless. They're cliqueish. As a social factor, they're very weak.' Other critical remarks were directed at specific activities. For example, a young man whose mother attended the tombola session remarked with feeling:

I can give an opinion of the tombola. I don't think very much of it. It's just jumping on the bandwagon because everyone else does it. People don't give any thought to the needs of the parish. I think it's rather cheap and I disapprove of it. I'm not against tombola, but against it being run by the parish.

The remainder approved of some activities but were critical of others; for instance, one person answered, 'I think they're all good things. The only thing I'm against is the Mothers' Union. It's not a cross section of parish life.'

Organization of the Parish

Views on the way in which the parish was organized reflected a similar trend. The number of those who said they did not know enough to comment was halved, however. One or two who had little knowledge made cautious remarks, such as:

Since I'm out of touch, I can't say. I would say it's as average as any of the parishes. That's all I can say.

Favourable views on the way the parish was organized were slightly fewer than they were on parochial activities, and some who expressed such opinions had little contact with the social life of the parish. This was the case with a university student, away during term, who answered:

It's better than most as far as the services are concerned. I haven't been to any parish superior. Socially, I don't know much about it. I've never heard anyone complain, from a negative point of view. It's praised quite a lot.

More of the remarks were critical, 35 per cent of the answers containing unfavourable opinions on the organization of their parishes. These comments were usually made in very strong terms. An instance was:

It's like any organization—good for people in the know. I've a very poor view of the parish. They all seem to be church collectors or people who pass the plate round. I don't take any notice of the parish or attend any of its functions.

Twelve per cent of the replies contained both praise and criticism. A young teacher, who, like other members of her family, was engaged in several activities in her parish, had this to say:

In some cases, it's very good, in others shocking. Some are well run, where there are one or two in charge. In others, there are a lot fighting for the top place. When the committee's well organized, it's all right.

The young man who had not wished to answer a question on his religious views also refused to answer this question, although, in fact, his opinion was revealed in the way he spoke:

Well, I won't go any further. As I said before, I have some views on this and don't want to go on.

Once again, there was a prominent dislike of organized activities which was echoed in a number of interviews with young men from different schools and different parishes. Many plainly felt that they had no need of a formal structure to help them make friends; their own interests were already well developed without the need of an organized social life. After answering this particular question, one young man went on to inquire:

Do you find other people like to go to clubs, that they like organized activities? I find my friends dislike organized activities or any authority. We disagree with most of them. We benefit from our group being loose knit.

Proposed New Activities

Nearly half had no suggestions to make for new activities in their parishes. Thirteen per cent said openly that they could not answer the question because, as one of them put it, 'To be quite honest, I'd better not say anything in case they have it.' Although so many said they had no proposals to make, this cannot be interpreted as a sign of satisfaction with the existing facilities. From the tone of the replies, it seemed more likely to be an indication of lack of interest. A remark typical of such answers was, 'I could probably cite a few— but I wouldn't go myself.'

Just over half took some interest in the question. Youth clubs were the most popular suggestions. One or two mentioned organizations to which they had belonged at school or at a Catholic college, and said they would join if a branch were started in the parish. But the majority wanted activities for other people, and it was often made plain that they themselves would not go. Even the youth club was intended for others. The following answers reflect this attitude:

I should like to see more dances for the young ones. I wouldn't go myself.
No, I don't think so. I've not much time for organizations and societies. But they should have a youth club.
They should have a Catholic Young Men's Society. I'm not interested myself, but they should have one.

It was interesting to see that in replying, many did not identify themselves with the parish by saying, for instance, '*We* should have a particular activity'; they spoke in terms of 'they', confirming the conclusion that they saw themselves as distinct from the sort of people who took part in parish activities.

'*The Ideal Parish*'

Concepts of what a parish should be were revealed to some extent when the replies suggested what facilities should be provided in 'the ideal parish'. Such views might be considered as forming a continuum; at one extreme, there was the idea that the parish was a community whose unity in religious worship expressed itself in its social life. At the other end of the scale was the view that the parish was a Mass centre for those living in the area. The opinions of the 11 per cent who said they often went to churches other than those in their own parishes seem to lie at this end. Similiar views were held by a girl who was born on the Continent of Europe; she contrasted the attitude to which she had been accustomed as a child with the strong regard for the parish as a social community held by many Catholics in Liverpool. She remarked:

I tend to think that church should just be church. I think perhaps there could be a few social activities—Catholic Action groups, too, I suppose. But I can't make up my mind whether I'm for or against them. The church is primarily a place for Mass and other devotions.

Thirteen per cent said flatly they were not interested. It proved impossible to probe further because it was evident that such people were adamant in their attitude, like the teacher who said firmly, 'I've never thought about it at all.' Amongst those people who had no personal interest in the matter was an agnostic who replied:

Well, you see, I'm outside now. From their point of view, now . . . I'd say occasional Days of Recollection or processions. Don't get them thinking.

All the others made some effort to answer the question. Fifty-two per cent named specific activities or organizations, trying to include the names of all the associations they thought should exist in a parish. These were mainly the groups usually to be found in an active parish. Others gave more general answers, suggesting, for example, that ideally all age groups should be catered for. Some of these answers approached the other end of the continuum, which stressed the idea of a social community as the basis of the parish. An active parishioner, for instance, replied:

It's too wide to state. Some religious societies, but only good ones . . . It should have some means of social life. After all, the early idea of the Church was that of communal life.

Other answers to this question seemed rather academic in tone, and it was evident that some were thinking again of activities for other people. Even some of those who took part in parish activities were not very enthusiastic in their replies, especially those who confined their participation to matters such as singing in the choir or serving on the altar.

The views presented by these young Catholics reflect considerable confusion about the nature of the parish. The idea of the parish which is being projected into contemporary society is, in fact, extremely amorphous. Theological and legal concepts have become more and more confused in people's minds by social activities.[1] Chapter 11 reveals how the pupils and former pupils of a parochial school have a concept of the parish which is very different from those current in the grammar schools. The additions which have been made to the basic parochial structure in attempts to adapt it to an urban environment have undoubtedly influenced this tangle of ideas. The social homogeneity of many parishes is disappearing, but it does not seem to be possible for activities, by and large, to transcend the barriers of education and social class.

Lack of Interest in the Parish

The prevailing attitude of the former pupils of grammar schools towards the parish can perhaps best be summed up in a remark made in one of the interviews:

I'm not really interested in the parish. The sort of things I'm interested in, it wouldn't matter where they were as long as they exist.

This comment describes the sense of irrelevance which many of the former pupils have for their parishes. The neighbourhood plays an insignificant part in their lives. They have learned to look beyond the parochial boundaries for friends and social activities.

This lack of concern was not confined to individual parishes, but to the parochial structure as a whole. Only one person, for example,

---

1. Some excellent points are made on this by A. M. Greeley, 'The Question of the Parish as a Community', *Worship*, XXXVI, 3 (1962), 136–43.

took part in activities in a parish other than his own. The way in which new activities were proposed confirmed this point, too. Sometimes it was visualized almost as an intellectual exercise; alternatively, suggestions were made on behalf of other people. Nor, with the exception of a handful of those who had lived in other parishes earlier in their lives, did they compare their own parishes with others; and as for the few who did, they usually made remarks about the priests, not the parochial associations.

Thus, the study of attitudes towards the parish reveals that the majority of the former pupils of Catholic grammar schools had little knowledge of parochial activities, and had even less interest. Few were actively involved in the social life of their parishes. Although 19 per cent took some part in parochial activities, only 11 per cent were engaged in several activities at the same time. The fact, too, that even some of those who were active were unenthusiastic about their parishes reveals the danger of assuming that participation in its activities is an indication of keen interest. Most of those who were interviewed saw the parochial system as irrelevant to their lives and the idea of membership had, in fact, made little impact on their behaviour.

It has been pointed out that lack of time is often given as the reason for the reluctance of former pupils to take part in parish activities. But although homework and other commitments probably had their share in forming attitudes towards the parish, it must be stressed that the investigation produced no evidence at all to suggest that the respondents' unwillingness was due to scarcity of leisure time. It was rare for those who were interviewed to imply that they could not afford the time to join parish organizations. As a rule, they did not even bother to make this point. It was plain that it was a basic lack of interest which prevented most of them from taking part in parish activities, and that they felt no sense of obligation to do so.

It is possible that this attitude is related to the age group into which those who were interviewed fall rather than to their educational experiences. To consider this hypothesis adequately, an investigation into the behaviour and attitudes of older men and women who had attended grammar schools would be necessary. Since this was beyond the scope of the present study, two other methods were used to test the validity of this argument. Firstly, parish priests were asked about the part grammar school parishioners, irrespective of their ages, took in the parish. The results are described below. Secondly, a study was carried out in a parish from which a high proportion of children went to grammar schools, and the findings are described in Chapter 11.

Views of the Parish Priests

In general, the parish priests who were interviewed confirmed the findings outlined above. They reported that few parishioners who had attended grammar schools took much part in parochial activities. Those who did so were usually engaged in several activities, and took a leading part in them, thus confirming the pattern of the multiple involvement of a few. Most parish priests referred spontaneously to the way grammar school parishioners of all ages were faithful to their spiritual duties, but complained that they found them little help in the parish. Some added that this was only to be expected because of homework while they were at school and other commitments later in life. Thus, the time factor was produced as the basic reason for failure to take part in parish activities.

But the age factor was not mentioned at all, except indirectly when it was said on a few occasions that young people had no interest in the parish. Evidently, the majority considered that reluctance to take part in parish activities characterized most of their grammar school population, regardless of age.

In only one parish did the pastor report that a considerable number of parishioners who had attended grammar schools were active. Significantly, this was a parish where a high proportion of children went to grammar schools. It would be worthwhile considering in detail the differences between parishes with a high proportion of grammar school parishioners and those with a low proportion.

Some parish priests reported that there were grammar school boys among their altar servers, but apparently even this was a mixed blessing. One priest said openly that they were a nuisance because they were not available to serve during the week and only came on Sundays.

The idea is often expressed that Catholic grammar schools should provide leaders amongst the Catholic population. The precise nature of this leadership is not usually defined, and it is clear that many of the former pupils are themselves uncertain as to what this means.[1] There is a continual emphasis upon the responsibility of educated Catholics towards the members of the wider society in which they live,[2] including their fellow Catholics who have not shared their educational privileges. The parish priests often interpreted this idea

1. In the Liverpool University Catholic Society, for instance, discussions often reveal confusion in students' minds between social leadership, through public life, etc., and the Christian idea that the leader should excel in the service of others. (John, XIII, 12–17, etc.)

2. Such ideas were expressed, for example, by Dr. John C. Heenan, formerly Archbishop of Liverpool, in his sermon to university students, graduates, and members of the University staff, at the annual Academic High Mass, in the Metropolitan Cathedral, November, 1961.

as meaning that those who received a grammar school education should take a leading part in parish life.[1] In their opinion, parochial loyalties should come first. The schools themselves, on the other hand, saw the matter in a wider context. As a result, the parish priests were very disappointed that only a handful of the former pupils was active in parochial activities. They felt the schools were failing to fulfil one of their major functions. Apparently, the confusion which exists over this is a source of conflict.

The ways in which the priests evaluated the situation were interesting. It was plain that considerably more was expected from those who had received a grammar school education. One pastor summed up these expectations in the following terms:

When any activity is proposed, it's very seldom I get any fair number of these people to give any assistance. But they help outside the parish. I'm very old fashioned, and no doubt expect too much. I think if there's scope at home in the parish, you should begin there . . . They're not inferior to the parochial school children, but the mentality is very different. The ordinary person won't say, 'This isn't any of my business.'

Another expressed a similar viewpoint, showing the stress upon the idea that those who received a higher standard of education had correspondingly greater responsibilities to the parish:

On the whole, you can't say they do much good for the parish. I don't say they don't practise their duties. But they don't take the share in parish activities which their education would permit. There are exceptions—a lot depends on the family. If they come from a good Catholic family, they probably will.

It seems, then, that the participation of parishioners who had attended grammar schools was evaluated in terms of an expectation which is considerably higher than that demanded from ordinary parishioners. The parable of the talents was often cited by parish priests to show that educated parishioners were at fault in not using their greater ability to the full. Responsibility was seen by them in a parochial context. Another point worth stressing is that most of the pastors saw their grammar school parishioners as a separate section in the parish, a group who behaved differently—although the patterns of behaviour and the expectations of behaviour did not coincide.

Factors Related to Parochial Participation

It has been emphasized that the majority of those who were interviewed lacked interest in the parish. But 19 per cent took some part in parish activities, and 11 per cent were actively involved. Why is it that while the majority rejected the parish as a means of social

1. A different approach has been made in the last few years by starting a course in Liverpool for young Catholics who have been to grammar schools to train as youth leaders. Here again, the stress is upon education producing responsibility, but this time it is interpreted beyond the parochial context.

interaction, others could nevertheless be sufficiently interested to belong to parochial associations? What factors were present in the experiences of those who took part which were missing in the lives of the majority? What were the influences which made them behave differently? When the results already described were considered in relation to the findings of other writers on the subject, four factors appeared to be relevant: family participation in parochial activities, education prior to going to a grammar school, occupation (including technical training or further education), and finally the length of residence in the parish. Accordingly, each of these factors was analyzed separately to see how they were related to patterns of participation and non-participation. In view of the small numbers involved, conclusions can only be tentative until further investigations verify or invalidate them.

Family Participation

This factor was the one which the parish priests continually stressed as most important, being most likely in their opinion to override the influence of the school. It is also reported by Ward to be the factor most closely related to parochial participation in St. Catherine's parish.[1] This proved to be so in the present inquiry; it emerged that all those who were engaged in parochial activities of any sort came from families where at least one member took part or had taken part in parish activities in the past.

Attention was turned to past membership of parish associations to test this relationship further. For the moment, those who still took part in parish activities were excluded. The analysis then revealed that two thirds of those who used to belong to groups in the parish came from homes where other members of the family had been active at some time.

The relationship between family participation and both past and present membership indicates, then, that the part the family takes in parish activities is of fundamental importance in influencing participation in parochial activities. However, some who took no part in parochial activities also came from homes where members of the family were active. While the influence of the family seems to have counteracted that of the school for some, more had been apparently affected by ideas and patterns of behaviour learned through the school.

Education

There were indications in the interviews that some ex-pupils thought that only those who had been to the parish school would be likely

1. *Op. cit.*, p. 116.

to participate in parochial activities. One girl who was critical of the latter, for instance, in explaining why she herself did not attend parochial functions, claimed, 'They don't like grammar school girls at all.' Another explained why he took no part in parish activities in the following terms:

> The trouble is, I was only at the parish school till I was eleven, so there wasn't much opportunity to take part in any except altar serving—and that backed out—because I was whipped away to the grammar school.

Approximately two thirds of the participants had attended their own parish school before going to a grammar school. But it must be pointed out that half of the boys interviewed and just under half of the girls had attended their own parochial schools, and that most of them did not participate. As with the family, it seems that the relationship works only one way: those who took part had usually gone to parochial schools, but attendance at the schools was not enough by itself to make people do so. Bearing this and other evidence in mind, it is suggested that attendance at the parochial school influences later participation in parochial associations only indirectly, in that parish school pupils will have had greater opportunities to get to know other parishioners of their own age and will find it easier to join in activities with them. It is probably familiarity with others who are already members which is the important factor, rather than the more direct influence of the school. This point, of course, could also be applied to the question of family participation.

Occupation

This is a factor which might be expected to operate against participation in parochial activities. The occupations of those who were interviewed were described in Chapter 3, and it was thus made clear that most of them were studying in some way; a number were or had been away from home for a part of the year at universities and colleges.

However, occupation did not seem to be related to parochial participation as far as the present study was concerned. Several managed to be active even though they were studying at Liverpool University or at a college, and the same was true of a few of the young women who had lived in residential colleges for two years. The handful whose occupations did not involve further study or training were not active parishioners. Attention has already been drawn to the fact that lack of time was rarely given as a reason for not taking part in parish life.

Occupation, then, does not appear to be relevant. It must be stressed, of course, that the occupations of the majority were very similar in status, and this may account for the failure to discover any relation between occupation and interest in the parish.

Length of Residence in the Parish

The factor of length of residence in the parish proved to be particularly difficult to assess. The usual phenomenon of urban mobility was complicated even more by the age of those concerned. They had been small children during the second World War, and during that time many children were evacuated from Liverpool. It was occasionally mentioned that families had been bombed out of their homes and had gone to live with grandparents or other relatives; others had been evacuated to rural districts.

In interviews with parish priests in central areas, it was sometimes pointed out that parishioners with children at grammar schools often moved out of the parish. Some went to the City's new housing estates, while others bought houses in the suburbs. According to a recent survey in central Liverpool, some parents wish to leave the district because their children obtain a better education in the suburbs, and so have greater opportunities for social mobility.[1]

In the present study, 40 per cent had lived in only one parish. Only 12 per cent both took part in activities and had lived in their parishes all their lives. Thus, for 28 per cent, being resident in the one area had not led to any participation in the social life of the parish. On the other hand, with the exception of one or two who lived in recently opened parishes, no one who was active had lived in his parish for less than three years. It is possible, then, that length of residence operates in a negative way, in that it tends to exclude newcomers, but does not necessarily promote membership of organizations. There were occasional references in the interviews which seemed to confirm this point. A young man who took no part in activities, for instance, said:

In a parish like this, everybody knows everybody else. With us being slightly new, we didn't mix in freely.

Someone who took an active part, too, in speaking of the organization of the parish, held a similar opinion:

I think it's very good, but it's cliqueish. If you're not in the organizations, you're definitely out . . . You're only accepted if you've been in a long time . . . They don't accept people readily enough.

1. C. Vereker and J. B. Mays, with E. Gittus and M. Broady, *Urban Redevelopment and Social Change: A Study of Social Conditions in Central Liverpool, 1955–56*, Liverpool University Press, 1961, p. 77.

Impressions From School

It was clear in the course of the investigation that children are given every opportunity to develop parochial loyalties in the parish schools. Their priest is constantly to be found there, they are taken into the church frequently, and teachers who live elsewhere often attend the local services, especially on feast days, to encourage the children to take pride in their own parishes.

What of the grammar schools on the other hand? The consequences of lack of contact with the parochial clergy have already been described. How were the teachers' attitudes perceived? Was it generally felt that taking part in parochial associations was a desirable activity while one was at school? The formal or informal policies of the schools in this regard have already been discussed in Chapter 5, but it is also necessary to discover the impressions which former pupils had actually received, because their behaviour would be deeply influenced by them.

It was clear that the majority did not think they had been encouraged to take part in parochial activities. Only a handful were either sure or more or less inclined to think that their grammar school teachers had considered participation as desirable while they were at school. Many were surprised at the question, in some cases even amazed. Whatever was actually said, the impression most had gained was that participation was not a matter of any interest in the grammar schools. Nearly half said that the topic had never been mentioned at all. The emphasis was always on the school. As one person put it, 'They never mentioned it. They wanted you to do as much as you could for the school.' Twenty-three per cent said much the same thing, by replying that the staff had not been at all interested in the question. Another 13 per cent said the topic had not been mentioned, but were prepared to speculate as to the probable views which would have been taken if it had been, most thinking that their teachers would have been favourably inclined towards participation. Only a handful thought the staff would have objected.

Thus, the crux of the matter lay not so much in unfavourable or discouraging attitudes towards the parish, but rather in the stress upon the school, which has already been underlined in Chapter 5. One girl remarked:

In the Sixth Form they used to object strongly because it distracted you from your homework. Otherwise they weren't very much concerned with what you did outside school.

Few, it appears, felt that they had been actively discouraged; the majority had the impression that what they did outside school was their own affair. The emphasis was, however, always upon the school, and as a result, all out-of-school activities tended to recede into the background. So it was as a corollary of school activities, rather than by direct injunction, that most had come to disregard the parish.[1]

Conclusions

For the majority of the former pupils, membership of the parish had little meaning beyond that of a source of Mass and the Sacraments. They asked little more for themselves than that it should continue to fulfil these needs adequately. Some could see how it could play a more important part in the lives of other Catholics, and proposed ways in which this might be done. But even where the parish was seen as being able to perform the function of providing for the social as well as the spiritual needs of Catholics, most made it clear that they did not regard themselves as being 'that sort of Catholic'. Their own interests lay elsewhere, and they did not want any social activities to be provided for them.

The priests, too, saw their grammar school parishioners as a distinct section. They expected more from them in terms of participation in parochial associations and were disappointed at their failure to live up to expectation. Thus, the former pupils of grammar schools not only saw themselves as different from other parishioners, but were also perceived as different by their pastors.

There was, however, a small section, consisting of people who were involved in parish activities. The major factor contributing to this appeared to be the interest of the family, and consequent familiarity with those who belong to parochial associations; attendance at the parochial school, and length of residence in the parish also helped, by establishing regular contact with others. The influence of the family had been more important for a few than that of the school. Their old loyalties were stronger than the new ones they learned at grammar schools. But it must be remembered that these people were in the minority.

For the majority, grammar school education seems to have resulted in a lack of interest in the parish and a general sense that it was irrelevant to their lives. Their educational experiences had left them without any sense of obligation or loyalty towards the parish. While this might be viewed with approval by some, including a few of their teachers, as being a sign that they understood membership of the Church in wider terms than those of local loyalties, others do not view the situation in this way. Their parish priests, for example,

1. The writer has developed this argument in 'Grammar School versus Parish', *The Clergy Review*, N.S., XLVIII, 9 (1963), 566–75.

expect them to fit into the existing structure; few seem to adapt to this situation in the way their pastors would like. Far from providing leaders of parochial life, as some parish priests would wish, grammar school education appears to be having disfunctional consequences for the parish. The old traditions associated with it have little or no place in the lives of these Catholics who have been to grammar schools. New ideas about the Church and Her social groupings are being transmitted to them through the educational system, and they find it difficult to relate them to the parish. For most, the gap between the old ways and the new is too wide to cross. The majority do not even wish to bridge it. For a few, family ties and the continuation or resumption of old friendships with earlier class mates from the parochial school draw them back into the parish on leaving school. But many have neither of these experiences, and others who have them reject them in favour of new ways of behaving. The increasing numbers of grammar school pupils makes their position a strong one, and widens the division between the old traditions and the rapidly developing new trends.

Chapter 8

THE UNIVERSITY 'PARISH'

THE social institution of the University Catholic Society is particularly relevant to the present study because it is an attempt to cope institutionally with new needs.[1] It is the formal recognition of the fact that increases in the numbers of young Catholics attending universities in Britain involve processes of social change which will produce corresponding changes in religious needs.[2] A young person's knowledge of his faith needs to be developed, and its social consequences understood, at the same time as his ability in other directions is realizing its potential. The conventional description of the 'faith of the Breton peasant' is, for instance, inadequate in the university setting. As the student's intellectual capacity grows in the university, so too his religious life needs to be deepened. In most universities in Britain at the present time there are Catholic Societies, and these are intended to fulfil for students much the same function as the parish performs for the general body of Catholics, offering as they do facilities for religious worship, the development of one's religious knowledge, and opportunities to meet other Catholics. The establishment of such Catholic Societies thus represents an attempt to adapt the social structure of the Church institutionally to social change.

It was, then, essential to consider in detail the precise nature of the institution of the Liverpool University Catholic Society; and then to discover how the university students who were interviewed evaluated it, and what effect it had on their behaviour. In this way, it was hoped to discover how far the experiment had been successful.

The methodological principle which governed the whole study, namely to obtain the views of those who were involved in the situation, was carried out in this section. All the following were therefore interviewed: the university students concerned; the chaplains of the Catholic Societies at the universities of Manchester, Leeds, Glasgow, Durham and Liverpool, the last on several occasions; and finally, the officers of the Liverpool University Catholic Society. Various

1. An edition of *The Dublin Review*, No. 484 (Summer, 1960), contains papers discussed at a conference of Catholic university teachers in September, 1960. A number of these, particularly P. Black, 'The Religious Scene. Beliefs and Practices in the University', are relevant to the present theme. Also the chapters relating to universities in *Catholicisme Anglais*, *op. cit.*
2. *Catholics in the Universities*, *op. cit.*

meetings and functions at Liverpool were attended throughout the study, and numerous informal discussions were held with members in various years concerning the issues raised. Catholic students who were not members of the Catholic Society were also interviewed, for their views were most important in this context. The chaplain at Liverpool was kind enough to permit access to the programmes of the Society dating back to 1932, and to the numerous publications issued by or referring to the Society throughout the years; these were an invaluable means of understanding how the Society had developed.

It might be added, too, that as the author was a member of the Society at Liverpool for six years, she was already familiar with its work, and understood why certain ideas had been developed and how others were rejected during that time. Going through the normal processes of membership, then, provided a good deal of insight.

The University Catholic Society

One of the clearest descriptions of the University Catholic Society is that of a former chaplain, who dealt with the salient points in the following questions:

Is a University Catholic Society anything else at all than the Church in the University? If Catholics form a local community, is that any other kind of community than those St. Paul addressed as the 'Church that is at Corinth, the Church that is at Ephesus'—churches, be it noted, incomplete and un-established if they were without their chaplain, their appointed priest?[1]

The analogy with the parish, then, is evident. The Catholic Society is to be the visible expression of the spiritual unity of the Church, 'the Church in microcosm'. Unlike the territorial parish, however, it is to be the Church in a social *milieu* rather than in a geographically defined area, an immensely important distinction, as will be seen. As with the parish, the appointment of a priest is the crucial factor in determining the status of the community in the eyes of the Church; while this is initially a theological matter, this will obviously have an effect in the social sphere.

It is clear, however, that the idea embodied in the University Catholic Society is still developing and that originally it had not been given so much prominence. To discover the ways in which its work has expanded as the needs for its services have increased, attention is given to describing the growth of the Society in Liverpool, where it has existed since 1913. Before 1942 the purpose of the Society was to provide a bond of union amongst its members, to promote lectures on religious topics, and to organize social functions. Religious

1. V. Wilkin, *The Nature and Aims of a University Catholic Society*. (Privately printed.)

services were occasionally held in neighbouring churches. The President wrote in the programme for the session 1938-9:

The Catholic Society at the University seeks to offer to Catholic students a cultural and social training in accordance with the precepts of their faith, and to awaken them to a full appreciation of their responsibilities as educated Catholic men and women.

These functions are still characteristic of the Society today, but its activities were considerably widened in 1941, when a group of young graduates took the initiative and established a Chaplaincy. A loan from the Society of Jesus (later repaid by the archdiocese) enabled them to purchase a house in the middle of the university precinct, and a Jesuit was appointed as the first resident chaplain. Until then there had been no resident Catholic chaplain in any university other than Oxford and Cambridge. In 1941, the chaplain wrote:

It is clear that every student, in order that he may be given a formation, social and intellectual, that is Catholic while he is at the University should have all the facilities that can be made available for the further study of his religion simultaneously with his secular studies. For nearly thirty years it has been the object of the Society to provide such facilities.[1]

Since that time the nature and functions of the Catholic Society have been greatly developed, and rather similar views have come to be held in other universities where a resident Catholic chaplain has now been appointed. In 1959, out of a total of twenty eight universities and university colleges in Britain, there were eleven with resident chaplains, some of them secular clergy, as is now the case at Liverpool; others, in Leeds and Glasgow, for instance, were members of religious orders such as the Jesuits. At Liverpool, as in the other universities where there are full time chaplains, the religious welfare of the Catholic students is regarded by the Archbishop as being the responsibility of the chaplain. The idea underlying these developments is that the students through their membership of the university form a distinct community, analogous to the parochial community. In this situation the chaplain assumes in many ways the role of the parish priest. The chaplain at Liverpool summed up the present ideal of the Society in January 1961 by stating:

It is not merely an aggregate of individuals who describe themselves as Catholic and who happen to be at the university. It is the visible expression of the Catholic Church in the university.

Thus the concept of the Society has expanded considerably since its beginnings, and the matter is still under discussion, the status of

1. J. Ryland Whitaker, *Foundation of a Resident Chaplaincy*, 1941. (Privately printed.)

such organizations altering as social conditions do. Much of the work of the Catholic Societies is experimental, since attempts are still being made to discover how best to meet the religious needs of the growing numbers of Catholic students.

Since many Chaplaincies are referred to as the university 'parish', it is important to note that the use of this term has no legal standing in the Church. The Code of Canon Law states:

Each diocese is divided up into distinct territorial divisions, and to each division its own church with a limited population is assigned and also its own pastor with the care of souls within that division.[1]

It is expressly forbidden by Section 4 of the same Canon to establish parishes on any other than on a territorial basis without the direct permission of the Holy See.[2] At the present time, therefore, the Chaplaincies are referred to as parishes only by analogy.

There are important consequences in this for the legal status and powers of the chaplains in Canon Law, and it was interesting to see that application was being made at the time of the fieldwork to the General Council of the Church, starting in October, 1962, for university chaplains without territorial parishes to be given the status in Canon Law of 'personal parish priests'. This status, incidentally, belongs to the chaplain at Liverpool by direct delegation of the Archbishop.

At the same time as the importance of the university community has been stressed, the ideal that parochial loyalties should be discarded temporarily has now been formally stated. Dr. Heenan has constantly emphasized this point in talking to students. For example, at the annual Archbishop's reception held by the Catholic Society in 1961, he drew attention to the necessity of leaving aside loyalties to one's home parish in order that the members could devote themselves to the responsibility of living a full life in the university. For the student, it is the Chaplaincy which is to be the 'parish'.[3]

It can be seen, then, that there is a carefully expounded ideology surrounding the institution of the University Catholic Society. The Society does not, however, exist in a social vacuum, and it is obvious that this policy of abandoning what may be considered to be previous parochial loyalties, but only temporarily, is one which is bound to encounter certain problems. No matter how well disposed a parish

1. Canon 216, Section 1.
2. Parishes on a racial or linguistic basis are examples of precedent in the granting of permission to found parishes which do not form a territorial area. Cf. J. E. Ciesluk, *National Parishes in the United States*, Washington, 1944.
3. A very different approach is adopted by the Methodists at Liverpool University. They wish the student to be part of a local church community.

priest may be towards the University Catholic Society, he may at times find it very difficult to refrain from asking one of his student parishioners to help him in some activity or other. Such incidents have occurred, and while some students have reluctantly refused because they believe their responsibilities to the university take prior place, others have either been unwilling or found it difficult to maintain this attitude when confronted with a real need in the parish. Such a dilemma may represent to the individual student a conflict of loyalties to his home parish and to the university. The fact that many parish priests and Catholics are totally unaware of the ideology that university students should 'leave aside' parochial loyalties aggravates the situation.

Students' Activities

It is now necessary to find out the extent to which the ideology of the University Catholic Society is understood and accepted by Catholic students as a whole. As many as 30 per cent of all those interviewed were students at Liverpool University (or had just left) and were living at home. Another three students were living at home while studying at Manchester. The university students represented 46 per cent of the total interviewed. Another two respondents had attended universities but had left after failing examinations; information was collected from one of these about the University Catholic Society, but the other had left after a very short time at the university, and had not been a member of the Catholic Society, so no information about the Society could be obtained from him.

Before asking about the Catholic Society, the interviewer dealt with university activities in general, in an endeavour to estimate the importance of the social life of the university, and also to discover how those who were interviewed saw the Society in relation to other groups. Almost all the students took part in voluntary social activities. Only three belonged to political organizations in the universities, and it might therefore be supposed that politics were not a matter of active concern to the majority. But it is difficult to draw conclusions of other than a specious validity from the information given in answer to this question. With a few exceptions, all respondents named various organizations or activities in which they took part, but in some cases membership was apparently nominal. This was particularly true of faculty or departmental societies of which membership in Liverpool is compulsory. The extent to which students participated in the activities they mentioned varied enormously, and requires more detailed investigation. No further attempts to analyze the answers to these questions will be presented because of the complexity of the replies.

Knowledge of the Catholic Society

All the university students were attending or had attended a university in which there was a Catholic Society, and all were aware of this fact. All said that they had some knowledge of the Society concerned, but some qualified this statement either at that point or later on. Only one student had no recollection of where he had obtained his initial information about the Society. The source given most often was that of notices or other publicity. An example of this was the Freshers' Conference, when in some universities the Catholic Society, like other organizations, has a stall in the Students' Union.[1] A typical comment of this type was, 'At the Freshers' Conference we were bombarded with leaflets'. (O)

Others had first learned about the Society when they were at school, through the initiative of the Chaplaincy. In Liverpool, the policy of the Catholic Society is to invite prospective university students from the local Catholic grammar schools to the Chaplaincy after the General Certificate of Education examinations are over. This gives them an opportunity to meet the chaplain and members and to hear about the Catholic Society. During the course of the fieldwork, the interviewer attended this informal reception. Members of the Society had volunteered to be at the Chaplaincy to meet the guests. The latter were then divided into small groups, usually according to their intended subject of study, and shown the department concerned and other university buildings. Afterwards all went to tea in the Students' Union where the Chaplain talked about the aims of the Catholic Society and its activities. During the afternoon, members of the Society chatted with the visitors and answered questions put to them about university life in general, and about the Catholic Society in particular. Special attention was given by the members to try to dispel erroneous impressions held by some of their guests, as, for instance, that the Society was an attempt to keep them together in a tight community as they felt they had been at school.

This introductory welcome apparently had the effect one would expect upon membership. Later in the same year many of the students who came to the Chaplaincy in their first term mentioned that they had been to this reception. They often remembered the students who had shown them around the university. Some of the guests, of course, went to other universities, and some failed their examinations and so were not admitted as students.

Others interviewed mentioned that they had heard about the

1. The excerpts quoted in this chapter are described as (L) to indicate that the students were at Liverpool University, or (O) to indicate that they were at another university.

Catholic Society through their friends. The importance of friends or acquaintances already at university seemed to be a vital factor in forming early attitudes towards the Society. Some who had learned about the Society when they were at school had been given friends' impressions, as the following answers show:

I knew about it before I went to University, from friends. I knew it existed and I had a vague idea of what it was like. (L)

I'm not sure whether it was mentioned at school before I left. But there were two old boys from school and they took us under their wing for a while. (O)

I went to — school. Our school *was* the Catholic Society when we came up. When we first came up it was very dead. (L)

It was interesting to discover that only two said their knowledge of the Catholic Society came through their own initiative, although their answers implied that they had previously been informed of its existence. A girl at Liverpool replied:

We just went to the Catholic Society. We regarded it as a duty. We were pretty regular members. (L)

Similarly, a young man studying away from home answered:

It was just one of the first things I looked up when I got there. I don't know really why now. Probably because of coming up from school. It's a place to meet people. (O)

The initial notices and invitations are followed at Liverpool by letters inviting students to the Chaplaincy. One person commented:

We were told before we went up. I was sent little notes. It's a good idea really. You tend to let things slide when you come up . . . There's so much else on your plate. It never occurs to you to go unless you make a point of it. (L)

The chaplain also appeals at regular intervals throughout the year after the daily Mass, and especially after Mass on Holydays of Obligation when more are present, for students to make contact with the Chaplaincy. Members also encourage friends to come along, so there are frequent attempts to inform and remind Catholic students of the existence of the Chaplaincy.

It was noticeable that although some said they took no part at all in the activities of the Catholic Society, only a handful said they had no knowledge of its activities. This contrasted sharply with the acknowledged ignorance of many concerning parochial activities.

Activities of the Catholic Societies

Although all Societies offer certain basic or main activities, some are able to offer others which are more extensive in scope, especially where resident chaplains have been appointed. In all the universities concerned there were opportunities to hear Mass, although not necessarily every day. In Liverpool, Mass is celebrated daily at lunchtime by the Chaplain. Although there is a small chapel in the Chaplaincy itself, this is not used for daily Mass because of its size, and the recently opened Cathedral Crypt has been given to the students as the University Church. At the time of the fieldwork, about eighty to one hundred students attended this Mass each day during term, the numbers increasing sharply during the penitential season of Lent.[1] On Sundays, Mass is celebrated at 5 o'clock in the afternoon and is attended by both students and staff. The chaplain gives a short conference lasting about ten minutes to a quarter of an hour. He described the purpose of this conference as being:

To give intensive dogmatic and moral teaching within the framework of the Sunday act of worship of the University community. It is meant to be an advance on the necessarily simpler catechetic instruction given in the average parish church, and more suited to the needs of the student.

With the establishing of a Sunday Mass in an increasing number of universities, more efforts are being made to point out the importance of the university 'parish' and of the students' responsibility towards it. The Sunday Mass is plainly a way in which students are physically removed from their parishes. It may be for some the breaking of the only remaining relationship with their home parishes. By discouraging the general public from attending the university Mass, further attention is drawn to the idea of the university forming a distinct community within the wider society. It may be worth adding, too, that as a result many find it difficult during vacations to overcome the strangeness felt at Mass in their home parishes. At the university, they grow accustomed to liturgical adaptations, such as the Dialogue during the Mass (that is, the people responding instead of through a server); also, the Epistle and Gospel are read in English by a student while the priest reads them in Latin. To return to a parish where none of these innovations is to be found may make a student even more critical of his parish and his pastor.

The services of Benediction and Compline were also mentioned by students from universities other than Liverpool, but in general the religious services were apparently taken for granted and were not mentioned in the interviews.

All the Societies hold lectures, usually by guest speakers, and discussions on religious topics are also regular items on their programmes. The extent of the social activities vary. Most of the students

1. It is impossible to discover the exact number of students who are Catholics, but at the time the numbers were estimated by the chaplain at about six hundred.

reported that the Societies arrange teas and occasional dances. In some Societies, including Manchester and Leeds, sporting activities, such as football, are a part of the programme. At Liverpool, on the other hand, the policy towards sports is different, the chaplain considering that those who wish to take part in them should do so as members of the Guild of Undergraduates.

Small Groups

In some universities, of which Manchester is a particularly conspicuous example, there is an increasing stress upon the development of small groups within the student body of the Chaplaincy. This tendency clearly increases the growing similarity to the parochial structure which contains a variety of organizations within the wider framework. Some of these groups in the universities are branches of highly organized associations which also exist in the parishes, such as the St. Vincent de Paul Society, the Legion of Mary or the Sodality. Membership of such organizations is formal, and involves precisely formulated obligations. Others are discussion groups of a more fluid kind, based sometimes on the members' studies, such as discussions on medical ethics, and sometimes on broader aspects of Catholicism in relation to university life. The numbers in such groups tend to be small, but the majority are flourishing, and the members are active and enthusiastic.

It is interesting, then, to see that as the Societies grow larger and it becomes more difficult for everybody to know all the other members, the need increases for small groups which make 'face to face' contacts possible. In 1961 a most ambitious scheme was produced by a group of chaplains and students. Its purpose was to give a basic introduction to university life and to provide an opportunity to discover through group discussion its relevance to the life of the Christian. Several such groups are functioning at present in Liverpool.

Students' Participation in Catholic Societies' Activities

Students were asked if they took part in any of the Catholic Society's activities rather than if they were members, since the writer was well aware from experience as a committee member that the two were by no means synonymous. Some replied that they did not, but later answers revealed inconsistencies, due again to the ways in which 'taking part' was interpreted. Because of these inconsistencies and the complicated patterns of participation, frequency of participation seemed a more reliable criterion of involvement than the enumeration of activities, for this question was answered unambiguously. A quarter said they did not go to any meetings at the time of the fieldwork. Some attended meetings only occasionally. Examples of such answers were:

Not really. Not very many of them. I occasionally go to tea. (L)

Not very many, I'm afraid. I found it was too big. It's a little bit cliqueish at the top. And also I came home at the weekend. I've a social life of my own here. (O)

It was noticeable from the answers that a small number attended meetings several times a month and took part in most of the Society's activities. Answers were on the lines of 'Yes, all of them' (L), or 'Most of them' (O). So once again the pattern of the multiple involvement of a few emerges. Only 12 per cent of the university students interviewed could be described as actively involved in the life of the University Catholic Society.

This phenomenon of the active nucleus was confirmed by regular observation at Liverpool, and the chaplains interviewed also agreed that there was usually a small section of members, involved in most of the activities, who used the Chaplaincy a great deal. This situation appears, as would be expected, to be a source of misunderstanding on the part of both the active section and of those who come only occasionally. The former complained that their attempts to welcome new members were frustrated by lack of co-operation, while the latter affirmed that the Society was run by cliques, a term very widely and somewhat indiscriminately used within the Chaplaincy at Liverpool.[1]

Attempts by the chaplain and members to deal with this problem at Liverpool have been many and varied. They appeared to be meeting with some degree of success, notably among younger students. However, the influence of older students in conveying their own unfavourable impressions has already been noted; this factor, which one would expect in any circumstances, is probably all the stronger in the present situation because of the extent to which the former pupils of Catholic grammar schools in the city attend Liverpool rather than another university, and because of the degree to which they are in informal contact with one another, a matter which is discussed at length in Chapter 10.

Opinions on the Catholic Society

Approximately half of the university students interviewed held favourable opinions of the Catholic Society's activities, although some of them were not active members. Examples were:

1. A similar picture is described in relation to parochial organizations by Ward, *op. cit.*, and other writers on the parish.

I think they're very good and well organized. (L)

They're quite good. They're much better run than parish organizations. There are more opportunities for discussions. (O)

They're a very necessary part of university life. They're quite good for people who can get to them. But something should be done about the Science students who aren't free at the time of the meetings. (L)

Some of these favourable comments were rather cautious in tone, as they had been in the case of the parish. One person, for instance, replied, 'They seem very good. I'm not fitted to make criticisms.' (L) Another answered rather ambiguously, 'I suppose they're the best that can be managed.' (L)

Twenty-six per cent gave replies which were critical, an example being, 'I think they are too much confined to Catholics and make absolutely no impression on the majority of students who are non-Catholics.' (L) A few were unwilling to make any comments, and others gave mixed views.

Another attitude which was expressed in discussing the parish was also discovered in relation to the Society, namely, the idea that the function of the Church's institutions was solely a spiritual one. One person put it this way:

I don't see what else you can provide. My personal individual view is that nothing but Mass and Communion are important. The lectures are above your heads. (O)

While this view of the nature of the Church was far from being that of the majority, it was expressed too often for it to be dismissed as an individual phenomenon. The consequences of this are of fundamental importance to the study. Clearly with such an attitude, a person would be reluctant to take part in the social activities of any Catholic group.

There were indications that a few had felt a sense of obligation to attend meetings, which contrasted with the attitude of lack of responsibility towards the parish.[1] Examples of this sort of reply were:

I just knew it was one of the things you did when you went up. (L)

Being in university, I thought I ought to be a member of the Catholic Society. (L)

From remarks in answer to this and the other related questions it appeared that there were some whose attitude towards the Society was similar, although by no means as strongly expressed, to that displayed towards parochial activities; a general approval of these activities as 'a good thing' for other people. A typical reply of this sort was, 'I suppose they're all right for those who like them. They

1. Later research carried out by the writer in another university has revealed the same sense of obligation to join on the part of Catholic students.

don't appeal to *me*.' (L) Accompanying this view was the tendency to think that such activities were not really relevant to their lives, as in the case of one student who said: 'I didn't think it was very important.' (L)

Only two of those who did not take part in the activities of the Society stated that they had not been invited to do so. With the exception of another two who were unable to remember, the remainder reported that they had been asked to take part, either by letters from the chaplain, or by their friends. A variety of reasons were given for not taking part. Although some had expressed criticisms of the Catholic Society, it was rare for dislike of the Society to be given as the reason, although one student said that he 'didn't like the atmosphere, quite honestly.' (L) Lack of interest was given by 28 per cent. Another young man who no longer took part explained that he 'just lost interest. I dislike the whole principle of organizations. I found the same sort of discussion outside.' (O) Another student expressed the same idea by saying, 'I'm just not interested in clubs altogether.' He then went on to add, 'I came home most weekends. That's another reason why I never took any part.' (O). Lack of time was mentioned by several as the reason for not taking part in the Catholic Society's activities.

University and Parish

The idea that the Catholic Society existed to serve the needs of those living away from home, and was therefore a superfluity for students whose homes were in Liverpool, emerged unmistakably in the answers to several questions. Members of the Catholic Society who had tried to interest other Catholics in joining the Society confirmed this point on many occasions. It appeared that some students who were by no means hostile to the Society saw no reason for joining because they lived in Liverpool. Sometimes such students mentioned their involvement in Catholic activities outside the university. These conflicting loyalties to university and to friends at home were revealed in several answers, and represent a problem which is particularly likely to occur when students are living at home, as a noticeably high proportion of them do at Liverpool. One of the young men in giving his reasons for not taking part answered:

Time. I didn't do very much at all. Also there was a choice between the parish and the University. All my friends are in the parish. (L)

This conflict between the parish and the Society is one which might be expected, and it is a point which people tend to raise to explain lack of interest towards either institution. It is particularly important, therefore, to emphasize that the evidence collected in the course of this inquiry by no means implies that the university student gave his loyalty to either one or the other. Some took no part in either. In the case of the six university students who took any part at all in parochial activities, all except one attended some of the meetings of the Society.

On the other hand, if the students who took part in the activities of the Society several times a week are considered, it is significant that none of them took any part in parochial activities. It is possible, therefore, that those who were most committed to loyalties to the Society had accepted the responsibility of concentrating on the university. (It is also possible, of course, that the explanation is that parish activities did not attract them.)

Purpose of the Catholic Society

The formal concept of the Society has already been described. But what were the ideas of those who are intended as 'parishioners' of this new social institution? How do they look upon the Society? Obviously some attitudes were already revealed indirectly in reply to previous questions, and respondents were asked directly, 'What do you think is the purpose of a University Catholic Society?'

It can be said straightaway that the majority of the answers did not reflect either understanding or acceptance of the formal ideology. Most suggested several aims. An idea which pervaded many of the answers was the defensive concept of 'keeping Catholics out of trouble', a view which probably has its parallel in a different social *milieu* in the opinion that youth clubs exist to 'keep young people off the streets'.[1] It was thought that the purpose of the Society was to keep Catholics together in some way; over half of the answers made this point in one form or another. It might be argued that this was one way of expressing the idea of a Catholic community which is featured so prominently in the official ideology. A remark which came, interestingly enough, from a young woman who was not a member, made this explicit:

To maintain a Catholic community. Not just individual Catholics, but an interlocked group who know about one another. (L)

However, some of the answers of this type tended to be unfavourable in that students thought keeping together was undesirable or unnecessary, as the following example shows:

It keeps the Catholic population of the University together. Frankly, I don't see that it serves all that great purpose. Not as much as I would have

1. These defensive attitudes on the part of Catholics were under constant fire from the chaplain at Liverpool. Similarly, Leeds Catholic Society's programme for 1961–62 criticizes the inadequacy of such an attitude.

thought. The average student has his own parish. At times the Catholic Society is quite superfluous. It's ideal for foreign students who have no home here. (O)

What was particularly interesting in replies of this kind was the inconsistency in the appeal to the parish, whereas in answering questions about the parish most rejected it as a source of either spiritual guidance on the one hand, or companionship on the other hand. Clearly there was confusion in the minds of some over this, a fact which is hardly surprising in view of the different ideas put across in different contexts.

It was suggested by some that the function of the Catholic Society was educative, providing opportunities to develop one's religious knowledge at the same time as one's secular studies. The following excerpts show how ideas of this kind were expressed:

To help fill the vacuum of religion between school and university. Your religion does not keep up with your studies. The purpose is to help by discussions and lectures and meeting other Catholics with the same problems. (L)
I think the instructions from church aren't really the level the university student requires—says she who doesn't go! [i.e., to the meetings of the Catholic Society]. You could get into difficulties in discussions with non-Catholics . . . You could discuss them at the Catholic Society with the Chaplain. (L)

Answering the problems which Catholics might encounter in university was mentioned in many answers, and defensive attitudes could often be seen in such replies. Examples of this sort of response were:

As I said before, when you leave home, there's a greater chance of losing your religion. (O)
I suppose it's a rallying point for Catholics in university! It's useful to have a chaplain for advice. The university's a bit of a jungle really. No one cares. (L)

That Catholic students were educated to expect opposition to their beliefs could be seen from their answers. One young man, for instance, indicated this in his reply, which also contained the frequent cry of disillusionment from students about the intellectual approach they had expected to find at university:

I should imagine the main purpose is to uphold the faith of the undergraduate against the arguments of the intellectuals they're supposed to meet—which I've never met. It's mainly for people living away from home. (O)

Occasionally it was suggested that the Society had some function for non-Catholics—one person even went so far as to give this as the sole purpose. Other replies put forward the idea that the Catholic

Society provided a religious atmosphere in the university. There was constant emphasis, as earlier illustrations have already implied, upon the idea that one should select one's company carefully. In this connection the importance of a Catholic environment for people living away from home was again stressed, as the following example shows:

I think the purpose is more for people away from home who may get in with the wrong sort of people. They drift. The Catholic Society binds you together and you can discuss the problems you're faced with. You realize how little you know. You're completely on your own otherwise. It's very good to keep up your religion like that and keep in with the right people. People are very easily led. (L)

A similar idea, but evaluated differently, was put forward by a young man who described himself as an agnostic, though he had once been a member of the Society and had attended meetings.

From their point of view, to keep you from thinking about religion. They can keep close tabs on you. It's amazing how they split hairs. (O)

Most thought the purpose they had given was a valuable one. The majority added a comment, such as 'definitely' or 'essential', in answering the relevant question. Once again, there were references in the replies to those living away from home, as for instance:

It's most useful. Essential at university, especially when people come away from home. They may have no friends. (O)

A Liverpool student made the same point by saying, 'Most decidedly, because most people are away from home', and added, 'I'm at home, so I don't need the Catholic Society.' (L) Only a few did not think the purpose they had given was a useful one (obviously including the agnostic whose remark was cited). One person commented thoughtfully, 'I suppose so. No, I suppose it can't be or I'd go!' (L)

Proposed Activities

A further attempt to discover the concept of the Society held by the students was made by asking what activities they thought a Catholic Society should provide. Most seemed to assume that spiritual activities would be part of the programme, and only a small proportion included them in their answers. The majority suggested several types of activities. Opportunities for discussions or lectures on religious topics were mentioned by some, and as many proposed social activities of one sort or another. Only one student suggested sporting activities. Over a third answered the question by saying simply, 'The ones this Society provides.' In fact, the majority seemed to accept the pattern already in existence, occasionally saying that their own Society did not offer sufficient facilities for a particular form of activity they themselves regarded as desirable. This usually meant dances or similar opportunities to meet other Catholics, and from the tone of some of the answers, this probably implied Catholics of the opposite sex.

A few said that they did not know, and one young man's disapproval of organized activities was so strong that he thought that, on these grounds alone, there should be no Catholic Society. Although he was alone in the extreme degree of his views, other replies reflected the idea that in the opinion of some of those interviewed, the Society was superfluous. One young man's answer which illustrates this showed again the appeal to the parish which had earlier been rejected:

A football team. Discussion groups can be done in your own parish. You've got your own priest. I suppose it's very good for people in digs and Halls of Residence. (L)

Contact with Other Catholic Students

Preliminary observation indicated that those who went to Liverpool University after leaving Catholic grammar schools in the city seemed to know many people of a similar background. Even those who left Liverpool to study away appeared to be in contact with other Catholics. It was expected therefore that all the university students interviewed would know other Catholic students.

This proved to be true. Though the schools were frequently the initial point of contact, the Catholic Society was also mentioned, but a large proportion had met other Catholics in their own departments or around the university. Several, for instance, had met other Catholics on the football field. They were quick, it seems, to identify one another. It appeared from both the interviews and from additional evidence collected from students that many Catholics met one another through school friends. It was this kind of contact which was often decisive as to whether or not they took part in the activities of the Society. The following comments indicate the sort of replies which were given in answer to this question:

I know a whole lot from school. I bump into them. And from other friends who seem to make other Catholic friends. (L)

Not from school. Definitely from university. In talking to them casually, I found they were Catholics. (O)

Most of them at school. In our particular year there were five out of twenty-five from our school. Then I knew friends' friends. And the football team. (L)

Reasons for Others' Lack of Interest

Questions were asked about the participation of these Catholic friends and acquaintances in the activities of the Society, and the

reasons thought to explain failure to participate. This was designed
to discover the views attributed to others, and it was hoped, too,
that through these comments a better understanding might be
reached of respondents' own attitudes. There were only a few who
said that all the Catholics they knew did take part. Lack of interest
was often given as the reason why other Catholics did not belong;
as these examples show, respondents' own attitudes were in fact
frequently revealed in their replies:

Apathy. Sheer can't-be-botheredness. (L)
They just can't be bothered. I don't take much part myself. (O)
I suppose it's the same as myself. They just don't bother. (L)

More than a quarter of the answers gave faults of the Catholic
Society as the reason for friends not taking part, which contrasted
with only three instances of this point for personal unwillingness.
Examples of this sort of answer were:

Because they're not really welcomed in the Catholic Society. I know when
we first came up, I used to go. Nobody would speak to you. You felt
awkward. Nobody made any effort to be friendly. (L)
When we came up, somebody went a couple of times. She said she was
lonely and no one spoke to her. I won't go myself. But I think it's changed
now. (L)

As the last comment shows, answers to this question again drew
attention to the crucial influence of friends in passing on attitudes.
One person summed it up by saying: 'I think to a large extent, it's a
question of whether or not your friends go really.' (L) Time was mentioned in a few answers, but the relativity of this factor was evident;
as another said:

I suppose those who don't go reckon they don't have the time, that it's
not important enough in their view. (L)

Other replies again reflected the idea that the Catholic Society was
not particularly important or relevant for those living at home. The
tone of the replies was significant, for it indicated that the refusal of
some people to take part in university activities was due not to the
apathy or perversity to which it is often attributed, but to conflicting loyalties. The following examples illustrate how a student may
see the situation:

I know the main reason why one didn't take part. He spent all his time in
his home parish. He was the head of a society. Other Catholics I know
went home for the weekends. They were in the choir in the parish. People
expect you to throw yourself into university as if you were in a vacuum. I
had all my friends already. It would have meant throwing them over. (O)

The majority are from Liverpool like myself and have friends in their home parish. There's no reason why they should take part. (L)

First Generation University Students

In considering the situation thus revealed, it seems worthwhile raising briefly the question of the first generation university student. At several of the meetings and conferences attended in the course of the fieldwork, it was noticed that special attention was drawn by those whose work brought them into close contact with Catholic university students to the fact that many Catholic students at the present time are the first members of their families to go to universities. In particular, at a conference on pre-university education, sponsored by Liverpool University Catholic Society, which was attended by head-teachers and others teaching at Catholic grammar schools on Mersey-side, members of the university staff, and students, several speakers pointed out that most students came from homes where the parents were unable to understand the problems which occurred at the university, including religious and moral difficulties. Similar opinions were expressed by students at a discussion in the Liverpool chaplaincy led by the headmaster of one of the schools included in the survey. This headmaster also emphasized these problems in a paper given as part of a discussion concerning the transition from school to university held by the University Staff Christian Group.[1] The chaplain at Liverpool also expressed concern at these difficulties. His comments on the religious problems which often arise in the students' homes were particularly interesting:

Often students who come from deeply religious backgrounds, but from homes where they are the first members to attend university, cause alarm at home by their frank discussion of religious difficulties, and their un-willingness to continue attending Mass and other religious services as a matter of routine. This is intensified by the fear that good practising Catholics of limited education sometimes have of the university as a place where religious beliefs may be destroyed. Even well-educated Catholics sometimes express their relief that their sons and daughters have made con-tact with the Chaplaincy, which they regard mainly as a defence. Any con-cept of developing and a deepening of religious knowledge which is only possible in the many sided atmosphere of a university is completely alien to many parents.

It is important to note, therefore, that roughly three-quarters of the university students interviewed were in the position of being the first member of their immediate family to attend a university. In the light of this fact, the attitudes of some of the respondents towards university life in general, and the University Catholic Society in par-

1. Rev. Brother Foley, *The Transition from School to University*. Unpublished paper, referred to by permission of the author.

ticular, become all the more explicable. The perception of the social activities of the university as a threat to relationships already established outside is an obvious instance of this.[1]

The Role of the Priest in the University

Reference has already been made to the question of the chaplains' legal status, and it must now be asked how far the role of the priest has been adapted to the changes which have been embodied in the reorganization of their Societies. It was found, in the first place, that the contact which the students had with their chaplains varied enormously. The chaplains do not visit parishioners' homes as the parish priests do. But where there are resident chaplains, they are normally available for much of the day in the chaplaincies; this characteristic feature of the institution of the University Catholic Society is one which distinguishes it from the ordinary parish. While this enables all students to see the chaplain as often as they wish, it also means that those who want to avoid him can do so, since he does not visit their homes.

Some students, after three years at their universities, reported that they had never met their chaplains. One, for instance, replied, 'To speak to, no. I've seen him in the Cathedral.' (L) Similarly, another young man remarked, 'No, unless it's the chaplain who says Mass at the Cathedral. I wouldn't know.' (L) The others all saw the chaplain at meetings, and some mentioned going to see him for a specific purpose. Those who did not go to meetings regularly were painstaking in their efforts to enumerate every such occasion.

The interviews revealed various significant differences between the responses to questions on the parochial clergy and the university chaplains. This is all the more noticeable when it is borne in mind that at no point in the interview were respondents asked what they thought of the clergy, but only how often they saw them. Although some comments were expected in planning the research, it was not until the fieldwork was completed that the importance of these remarks was fully appreciated. Thus all the information came from spontaneous comments, and it was remarkable that they were made almost invariably.

The first difference which emerges between the parish and the university in this respect is that in answering the questions about the parish, references were made to the parochial clergy in a very high proportion of the answers, though these were not sought, or even expected. Whether the comments were favourable or critical, all were

1. Jackson and Marsden, *op. cit.*, have already thrown much valuable light upon the general difficulties of divided loyalties which may be experienced by those who are the first members of their families to attend universities.

clearly aware of the dominant role of the parish priest. In the case of the University Societies, on the other hand, the only spontaneous references to the chaplain were made when a handful expressed the opinion that his presence was necessary to give advice; his role was apparently unobtrusive.

Secondly, although some students had never met the university chaplain, no one ever suggested that this was the chaplain's fault. As one of them put it, 'No—but I could have done.' (O) This was in sharp contrast to the complaints which were sometimes raised that not enough was seen of the priests in the parish. The initiative appeared to rest with the layman in the university, but with the clergy in the parish, an important distinction.

Thirdly (and this is probably the most significant feature of all) only one critical remark was made about the chaplains. This came from a young man who said he was no longer a Catholic, and it was in fact more of a criticism of the Church than of the chaplain concerned. Clearly, this was vastly different from the criticisms made at times about the role of the parochial clergy.

As a result of the interviews and regular observation of the situation, it is suggested that these important differences in the replies can be attributed to the different role assumed by the chaplains in the Societies. The work of the priest in the university is comparatively new and is designed to meet needs which have developed comparatively recently. The role of the parish priest in Liverpool, on the other hand, developed in a different social setting, and is more regulated by tradition. Some of the attitudes of the latter seem to be a source of confusion and misunderstanding at times to young Catholics who have been to grammar schools, while the function of the priest in the university is apparently understood and accepted. A factor contributing to this is probably the fact that the chaplains are especially chosen and appointed for the work and are frequently graduates themselves; moreover, they meet regularly to discuss their work. It is worth noting, too, that some have never worked in parishes and so never experienced as priests the traditional parochial situation.

It was interesting to discover the extent to which the chaplains' advice was sought each day. All the chaplains interviewed stressed the importance of this aspect of their work, and it was plain from observation that a good deal of time was given to individual pastoral care. Thus, university students are ready to ask the priest for advice, but they look for it in a context outside the parish. What appeals to them, it seems, is the idea that the priest is there when they want him.

It is clear, then, that it is not the priesthood which is rejected, but only certain aspects of the role of the parochial clergy. In the University Catholic Societies, the role of the priest has evidently been restructured in response to changing social conditions, and there is every reason to believe that at the present time this adaptation is successful.

Conclusions

One part of the ideology surrounding the University Catholic Society was clearly understood by students: the new role of the priest was acceptable to them, and appears to be well adjusted to a changing social situation. But it appears that the ideal of the university 'parish' was understood by only a small proportion of the students, who, for the most part, had spent three years at university. It seems likely that one of the reasons why attempts to communicate this concept to students are frustrated lies in the influence of their friends and acquaintances who convey their own attitudes to younger students. For instance, at one period a few years ago, many of the active members of the Society had attended a particular boys' grammar school in Liverpool; although this had not been so for several years, it appeared that some students still held this belief, transmitted to them by older students, and it was reinforced by the fact they rarely attended meetings.[1] A similar phenomenon was reported by the chaplain to Catholic students at Leeds.

While the influence of friends appears to be an important contributory factor, a much more radical reason must be found to account for the limited impact which the university 'parish' makes upon students. The implications of remarks made in the course of the fieldwork suggest that this lack of response to the university 'parish' can be understood in terms of the concept that many of the students had of the Catholic Church. Although answers from some reflected an understanding of the social community of the Church, the majority stressed the spiritual union of Catholics. They looked to the Church for the Mass and the Sacraments, for spiritual and moral teaching and guidance, but not for formal social interaction. It is true that they often said it was necessary to keep in the 'right' environment, and to avoid the dangers of the 'wrong' sort of company. But for this they looked to other Catholics, that is, to individual members of the Church, rather than to the institutional framework of the Church. Many answers explicitly rejected the importance of social communities within the Church.[2]

With this picture of the Church in mind, the idea of the visible expression of the Church in the university is not likely to be immedi-

1. The year after the bulk of the fieldwork was completed, another school was reported to be dominating the Catholic Society at Liverpool.
2. It is suggested that this concept has much of its origin in the Sixth Form teaching on the nature of the Church, but this is a hypothesis which has yet to be tested.

ately meaningful to them. Moreover, these attitudes are probably un-wittingly reinforced by the constant stress upon the analogy with the parish. If they have never experienced the sense of a living community which has been proposed as the ideal of the parish, they are likely to remain unmoved by this appeal to something which many young Catholics at university have probably never seen in practice. The con-fusion of theological, juridical and cultural concepts surrounding the contemporary image of the parish makes it even more difficult to convey to university students the idea of 'the Church in the univer-sity'. By the present development of the University Catholic Society, and continual adjustment and revision of policies upon the basis of experience, efforts are being made to meet new needs. The structures and relationships which are developing may be appropriate to a Christian community, but they have little in common with the con-temporary notion of the territorial parish. Thus, instead of the con-stant references to the parochial community making the University Catholic Society a more intelligible concept, they probably only succeed in identifying it with a structure which students have often already rejected. It has been pointed out that their answers were in-consistent, because they sometimes expressed acceptance of the parish and rejected it shortly afterwards.

It seems, then, that at the present time the attitudes of these students are in conflict with both the territorial parish and grouping in the university. It must also be remembered that these young people are in informal contact to such an extent with other Catholics, and have become so accustomed to this, that the community which they form probably does not strike them as—and may not be—a charac-teristically religious one. It also seems likely that the situation is ag-gravated by the confusion which exists at present about the extent to which the university should be a community by itself. Opinion on this differs immensely and the whole matter is itself a subject worthy of intensive research. But clearly many Catholic students in Liverpool mix a great deal with friends outside the university, and there is evi-dence to suggest that at least some fiercely resent attempts to place them in a special category. In some ways they perceive the stress upon university activities in general as a threat to the relationships they have known outside, both with members of their families and with friends. Clearly, some of the values and ideologies surrounding the university and the University Catholic Society are in conflict with those held by Catholics outside the university. Annoyance is often expressed, for instance, at the reluctance of university students to help in organizing both parochial and extra-parochial Catholic activi-ties, which they are being urged in another context to disregard tem-porarily. The 'allegiance' of the Catholic student at such a university as Liverpool may, indeed, be interpreted in a variety of contexts in a corresponding variety of ways.

Thus, the attempt that has been made to cope with change institutionally is sometimes frustrated because other policies of the Church conflict with it, and partly because old attitudes inherited from earlier social systems still linger on. Moreover, the idea that the Church may exist in a social *milieu* as well as in a territorial region may well be generally accepted in the future, and if this is so, the social divisions already becoming apparent within the Church will be accentuated. The consequences of such a policy upon the attitudes of Catholics towards the parish are likely to be far-reaching. There is also another reason for these frustrations which are now being experienced, for the attitudes which many Catholic students have towards their religious beliefs further complicate the issue. It has already been said that there are some who see their faith as something to be protected. Some students, it seems from the interviews, were satisfied that their own faith was sufficiently well safeguarded in the company they kept, composed of Catholics like themselves. But they expected the Catholic Society to fulfil this function for others whom they evidently regarded as less fortunate. The institutional framework was of value, in their opinion, only when informal relations were lacking. This being so, it is hardly surprising that these students should, by and large, fail to grasp all the implications of a new spiritual and social community. This lack of understanding is reflected in the behaviour of the students who use the Chaplaincy to meet their friends, but do not realize the opportunities it offers them to develop a more mature understanding of their faith as they acquire more knowledge in the university. The chaplain has often complained of the way some Catholic students keep their religious beliefs in a separate compartment, without trying to develop them together with their other intellectual advancement. The increasing stress on the need to educate pupils in the Sixth Form in preparation for their university life indicates that this defensive reaction of Catholics towards the wider society has already caused some concern.

Perhaps the most interesting questions of all are those which the present study cannot attempt to answer: what happens when the students leave university? Are all the links with the parish broken, at least for the majority? Or does marriage and a family lead some of them to seek roots once more in the parish? What part does the older graduate play in the parish—and, a consideration which becomes more important as the number of Catholic students increases, what part will he play in the future? The findings of this research cannot but lead to speculation, and another inquiry is needed to answer these questions with any degree of finality.

Chapter 9

EXTRA-PAROCHIAL CATHOLIC ORGANIZATIONS

IT is already plain from the evidence presented in Chapter 7 that most of the ex-pupils of grammar schools did not regard the parish as in any sense important to them. But what of the many non-parochial Catholic groups in the city? Was it not possible that these groups, organized without relation to neighbourhoods, might attract young people who had attended grammar schools? Might not some of these have taken over functions once performed by the parish? It seems more likely that young people who had grown accustomed from an early age to going to schools away from their own neigh-bourhoods would develop loyalties and interests in a wider setting. Many of the extra-parochial groups were set up explicitly to meet needs which were not—or could not be—met in the parishes. Some, such as the former pupils' associations, have developed directly round the educational system itself; and others, such as the Newman Association, a body of Catholic graduates, are designed to meet new needs which have resulted from education. Consideration of the part such organizations played in the lives of the former pupils of gram-mar schools was, then, an essential step in the inquiry.

In view of the great number of extra-parochial organizations in Liverpool, attention is confined to those groups to which the people who were interviewed belonged or had once belonged. The focus is on the activities of these young Catholics, and the study in no way aims at describing all the extra-parochial activities organized by Catholic associations in the city.

Former Pupils' Associations

The obvious place to start this section of the inquiry is with the mem-bers of the former pupils' associations attached to the grammar schools; their experiences are relevant not simply because they had left school comparatively recently, and might therefore be expected to maintain links with the schools, but chiefly because it was clear that at least two of the schools included in the survey had associations which also catered for the former pupils of other Catholic grammar schools. For the moment, however, the discussion will be confined to members of the associations attached to the respondents' *own* gram-mar schools; the part they took in the activities of organizations attached to schools other than their own will be described later in this chapter.

Although most of the schools included in the survey had a former pupils' association attached to them, comparatively few of the respondents took an active part in their activities. Only 18 per cent were members, though another 10 per cent had once been members; one of the latter commented, 'I found it just didn't seem to be worthwhile. They still contact me. I'm rather pushed for time and money anyway.' Eleven per cent went to meetings although they were not members. One young man, for instance, said, 'Well, technically, no, but I play rugby for them.' Similarly, another replied, 'I haven't paid my sub but I go.' The remainder did not attend meetings at all. Some indicated their attitude to such groups immediately by the way they answered. One girl, for example, said promptly. 'When I'm fifty, I'll join!' Others had already made it clear that though there was an association attached to their school, they did not belong to it.

As some were only nominal members, frequency of attendance, as with the University Catholic Society, proved to be a better indication of involvement rather than simply listing the activities in which people took part. From this, it emerged that only 10 per cent took part in such activities once a month or more often. The remainder attended only rarely, usually for special occasions. It must be pointed out, moreover, that some of these associations met only two or three times a year, and clearly fulfilled a different function from, say, one of the associations which had its own premises. In the girls' schools, activities were largely confined to a few social meetings each year, with perhaps a day of recollection as well; one association which offered its members facilities for a variety of interests, including drama and sports, was, however, an exception. Again, though one of the boys' schools did not have an association at the time of the fieldwork, it started one later. The associations attached to the other two boys' schools offered extensive activities, particularly on the sports side.

Opinions on the Former Pupils' Associations

Most who had not belonged to an association had little knowledge of them; this was sometimes made very clear indeed, as by the respondent who said, 'I haven't the remotest idea about them.' Others might have partial knowledge, but did not want to give any opinion: 'I've never been to any of them', was the typical response of this kind. Nineteen per cent of the replies gave favourable views, but such answers tended to be cautious, as the following remarks show:

I'm not very qualified to comment. I think they're on a par with most of the Old Boys' Clubs in the district.
I suppose they're fairly typical.

Thirty-one per cent, on the other hand, were critical of the associations, and were less tentative in their replies. A young man, for instance, answered, 'Not very much except the religious side. You don't really gain anything.' The associations attached to the girls' schools came under sharper fire. The fact that their activities were different from the boys' schools has already been pointed out. What some of those eligible for membership thought of them is illustrated in the following replies:

It's very deadly. In the lower Sixth and the Fives, they used to ask us to go to the teas. When you looked round, it comprised last year's leavers and a sprinkling of the year before, and the old originals. They all sat in a little group. It was rather ludicrous.

Not satisfactory. It's only interesting if by chance there are interesting people there. There are a lot of old people and very young ones. They cut us out.

Some of the unfavourable remarks were aimed at organizations in general, a point which has already been made several times in relation to other activities, including the parochial. Examples of replies from young men who did not want activities to be arranged for them were:

As far as organized activities are concerned, I can't tolerate them really. I prefer to find my own entertainment. I'm not at all impressed by organized activities.

I've never thought about them. I'm certainly not interested in the Old Boys'. I feel there are more interesting things to do elsewhere.

I'm not really qualified to answer. Usually a certain type stops on. I'm not that type. I've neither the time nor the inclination.

Few of those who did belong had taken the initiative themselves. Usually people had drifted in, perhaps as the result of requests made in the Sixth Form, or through the associations' sports. The following are examples of explanations of how members had come to join:

I played rugby for the school, and it seemed natural to play for the Old Boys'.

When I left, I knew so many people. I thought it would be a good idea to keep in touch that way. In point of fact, you meet a lot outside anyway.

Not many had proposals for activities which they would like an association to provide. The fact that few suggestions were made was not an indication of satisfaction so much as a lack of interest, as it had been with parochial activities; the following extracts indicate this attitude:

No, not really. I wouldn't count it as my club. I don't know enough about it.

No, the primary purpose is to keep school friends together.

Not really. I'm not particularly interested.

Lack of interest, too, was the main reason for not belonging, or as one person said succinctly, 'apathy'. The following replies were typical:

I'm just apathetic. Nobody made any effort, so we didn't. There's the time factor, too.
Really, it's just apathy. I'm not interested. The thought puts me right off.
I'm a lazy type. I can't be bothered giving my name in.

A few replies mentioned lack of time, and criticisms of the associations also figured in the answers. Some mentioned that they had been away from Liverpool for part of the year. Dislike of the particular school, or of school life in general, cropped up occasionally, too, as the following comment shows: 'It just didn't appeal. I didn't know anyone who joined. I was glad to get away.' Those who reported (not always accurately) that their former school had no association were asked if they would have liked one. Some respondents were plainly not interested; as one of them put it, 'Not particularly. I associate with my own friends from school. I've not got the time.' Others viewed the suggestion with approval, but their interest was not necessarily a personal one, as the following responses illustrate:

It's a good idea, but I personally wouldn't be interested. I've got so many other things.
I think that it would be a good idea, but I wouldn't be interested. I think a lot of people would like to meet old friends. I was looking for something like that when I left school, but now I've got other interests.

The activities which were proposed for such an association followed the pattern of the existing associations, by and large. Evidently no one visualized the former pupils' associations playing an important part in Catholicism in the city.

Purpose of Former Pupils' Associations

By their comments, most had already given some indication of what they thought was the function of former pupils' associations. To obtain more explicit statements, they were asked what they considered was the purpose of such associations. The majority of the replies confirmed the idea which had previously emerged, that the predominant function was to offer leisure time facilities. Ninety-three per cent of the answers included the point that the purpose was to provide opportunities to continue friendships started at school; some evaluated this idea as they replied:

I suppose the idea is to keep you in touch with your old school friends. It's impossible to keep in touch with them all, and you'll see those you're friendly with anyway.
I think it's really to meet old friends. The girls who go aren't my friends.

Well, I suppose it keeps you in touch with your original friends from school. Personally, I can't see any purpose.

Some who thought this was the major function of the associations considered that the religious aims usually expressed in the constitutions were not fulfilled, as the following examples indicate:

It's mainly a social club. You join because practically everybody is somebody you know. I don't think the Old Boys' is any more than that in spite of the charter. People are not interested.

To keep the old boys in touch. It's a chatty sort of establishment. I think that's the purpose and no more.

However, some answers, 23 per cent in fact, did refer to aims associated in some way with Catholicism. Among these were some which were similar to the idea expressed in relation to the University Catholic Society, that such groups had a protective role. The following excerpts show the type of reply which was given:

In a way, to safeguard the social activities of Catholic former pupils. I suppose it's very easy to go off the rails. If you belong to the association, you mix with the same sort of people.

It brings everyone together when they have left, whereas you probably wouldn't bother. And I suppose for Catholics, it brings you in touch with the faith, for someone who is inclined to forget.

First, it's a Catholic organization to make sure that people keep in touch. We have a chaplain to make sure the faith is being kept. And to keep up with friends and old comradeship at school.

One thing is to keep the boys together. It's like a second home to them. And also it keeps them within their religion. A lot float off. It keeps them within the bounds. I know a lot of boys out of the forces who float around.

Most thought the purpose they had proposed was a useful one, usually adding a comment, such as, 'Yes, I'm glad of the opportunity to meet old pupils.' Some of these comments made reference to the religious factor; examples were:

Yes, especially if there is some religious instruction as well. People sadly lack this.

If you want to keep up with the school and a Catholic circle. From a Catholic point of view, it's useful.

It must be. We [i.e. the family] are all gathered up in Catholic societies. Lots of people aren't.

A few considered the purpose 'not so much useful as pleasurable'; as one of them put it, 'It's enjoyable, but not useful', adding, 'and it's only enjoyable for a few years.' Ten per cent did not consider such associations served any useful purpose at all, and were emphatic in their disapproval, as the following excerpts show:

I don't think so. I hate the idea of the old school tie.
No, not really. Quite pointless in a way. Maybe I'm prejudiced there. I was glad to leave the school. Or rather school life really. Not so much the actual school but the pupils.

Thus, although some took part occasionally in the activities of the former pupils' associations attached to their own schools, only 10 per cent did so once a month or more often. In some schools, activities were confined to reunions a few times a year, and the function of such associations was largely limited to offering opportunities for meeting school friends. Although this was appreciated as a useful function, the fact that most were already in contact with people who had been their class mates (this is described in the following chapter), made many of them view it as yet another form of activity for other people. Regardless of the organizations' stated aims, most saw them as being primarily related to leisure time. While functions associated with Catholicism were mentioned, these were often cultural rather than religious.

Other Extra-Parochial Organizations

It has already been said that there are numerous extra-parochial Catholic associations in Liverpool. Some are designed to meet the needs of a particular section of Catholics, the Liverpool circle of the Newman Association, a body of Catholic graduates, for example. Others, such as the Catholic Evidence Guild, were established for a particular purpose. Membership of some of these groups is open to all Catholics, but others, like the former pupils' associations, are intended to cater for the interests of Catholics who had attended grammar schools; the Catholic Metropolitan Club, too, comes into this category. In this inquiry, however, only those groups to which the respondents belonged will be considered. Excluding the University Catholic Society and the former pupils' associations referred to above, the majority of those interviewed, 74 per cent, said they took no part at all in Catholic activities outside their own parishes. In an attempt to include everything, people frequently mentioned relatively trivial events, such as having attended a dance on St. Patrick's Night, but it was clear that such activities were rare, and the very fact that such occasions could be remembered draws attention to their infrequency.

Eight per cent, all girls, belonged to some Catholic organization whose aims were primarily religious. Only two respondents had committed themselves to attending weekly meetings. The remainder confined their membership of Catholic organizations to the social or sporting side. Five per cent, for instance, were members of a Catholic sports club attached to one of the former pupils' associations, catering for those people who had attended other Catholic grammar schools, as well as for their own ex-pupils.

Past Participation in Extra-Parochial Activities

Just over half of those who were interviewed had taken part regularly in Catholic activities outside their own parish in the past; most had left because of their age or lack of time after leaving school. A variety of activities were mentioned, from sodalities to sports clubs, from dances to scouts. Many had at some time attended dances organized by the former pupils' association attached to one of the boys' schools included in the survey. Attendance at these dances seemed to follow a regular pattern, and it was found that this was a crucial factor in developing an awareness that there were other Catholics of 'the same sort' as themselves. Most appeared to have started to go to these dances at about the age of sixteen or seventeen, gradually stopping after a couple of years; although several people mentioned that they still went on special occasions, such as New Year's Eve. As one put it, 'It seems to be a tradition that every Sixth Former should go.' The following remarks, expressing views on these dances and the reasons for leaving, indicate the existence of this custom:

We were associate members purely and simply to get into the dances. Everyone cuts their teeth there.

When I was sixteen to eighteen, I enjoyed it. It was excellent. I really enjoyed it. If you liked a girl, there were no religious problems. I enjoyed the type of conversation. If I went after I was about eighteen and a girl asked me how many subjects I got at 'O' level, it was tedious. Between fifteen and eighteen, it was excellent. I think our school should start one.

At first, I thought it was marvellous. The boys were quite nice, and they were the same age and had the same interests. But the same people aren't there now. They're courting or in the forces or married. I go occasionally on gala nights.

I thought it was great. It was the only place I could meet other Catholics.

Several respondents added the remark that in their opinion, such activities could not really be termed 'Catholic'. In speaking of the dances described above, one person commented, 'It's not really much as a Catholic activity, except that you're sure of mixing with Catholics'. Another significant remark, made with reference to a sports club, was, 'I've never judged it from the religious side. It was just the same as other clubs.'

It is worthwhile noting that many had once belonged to a Catholic organization, often within the parish if one was available, in preference to a similar group organized without reference to religion. Parental influence was probably the determining factor for the very young, but at a later age people then seemed to have a general preference for a Catholic organization, such as a tennis club, as a matter of course. It simply did not occur to most to do anything else. After leaving school, the process seemed less automatic, especially with university students. As one of the latter said, 'It was only at university that I thought of mixing with non-Catholics.' At the time of the fieldwork, there were some who belonged to ordinary clubs and societies, especially at university. However, a few still preferred to belong to a Catholic club. It is possible that the question of finding a Catholic marriage partner was a factor influencing such decisions. Existing patterns of friendship seemed influential factors, too, a topic which is discussed in detail in the next chapter.

Catholic Organizations in Catholic Teacher Training Colleges

In Catholic training colleges, religious organizations of various types are normally present, and so those who had been students in such colleges were asked about membership. Only one person said that there had been no groups in her college. All the others reported that there were several, and more than a dozen associations were named. Most involved attending a meeting and performing some task each week. Those most frequently mentioned were the Legion of Mary and Our Lady's Sodality. Although the membership of such groups was optional, students were strongly encouraged to join them, and only a few had not done so. Some had joined a branch of the organization to which they had belonged in school. Apparently most had felt a sense of obligation to become members of an organization, as the following remarks show:

I thought I should join one, and that appealed the most.
Although it was optional, we decided we should join one because they were doing a lot.

Only a few had criticisms to make about these groups. Most replies expressed strong approval both of the way in which they were organized and the work they did. The following examples were typical:

They aroused great enthusiasm in college. I thought they were very good.
They were very well run and organized and did some good.
They all seemed to serve some very useful purpose. They had much more meaning than in school.

Yet in spite of this attitude, only three respondents had either continued their membership, or, in the case of those who were still students, intended to do so. Lack of opportunities for continuing membership where they had lived was mentioned as the reason by some; one girl, for instance, in explaining why she had left, said, 'It was only because the parish hadn't a group'. This was, however, a relative factor, since branches of every organization mentioned exist in the city, although not necessarily in all the parishes. Some, such as the Catholic Social Guild, are not parochially based in any case.

Occasionally other specific reasons were given, such as lack of time, but the others said simply that they had dropped their membership because they had left college. It was much the same process which took place with the school groups. It seems that membership was usual while at college, but that it ceased to be so after leaving; it was no longer expected in the way it had been at college. As one girl remarked, apparently with some degree of accuracy, 'When I came out of college, I stopped—everyone else did.' The remarks on the organizations showed that most accepted the obligation to belong to such groups without resistance or complaint, and that there were no indications that they rejected their aims and principles after leaving college. Yet only a few continued their membership. The rest appeared to be like the girl who said she had no particular reason for leaving, and added, 'It was just mainly because you go with a group from college when you go.' Even though some still went round with some of the friends they had had as students, they did not belong to branches outside college. The three girls who still remained members went to the meetings alone.

Chaplains at Catholic Colleges

In the Catholic teacher training colleges the role of the chaplain appeared to be much more clearly defined than in the schools. Some respondents did report, however, that there was no one holding the official post of chaplain in the college they had attended. Where there was a chaplain, the former students said that they had seen him frequently, often several times a week; he not only celebrated the Sunday and daily Mass, but also gave lectures, and acted as spiritual director to the religious organizations. Even where students said there had been no official chaplain, there was a local priest who came in regularly for Mass or to lecture. It appeared that contact with members of the non-parochial clergy was frequent while most of these students were at college.

Conclusions

It seems that none of the formal extra-parochial groups are identified for these young people with belonging to the Church. Only a few were actively involved in such activities. The former pupils' associations, for instance, were viewed by most as being predominantly concerned with leisure, and the majority made it plain that they did not want any structured or formal way provided for them to meet people after leaving school. Once again, they saw such activities as fulfilling a useful function for others.

However, some activities of these associations, such as dances, appear to have an important function for Catholics in the city, in that they give opportunities to the pupils and former pupils of grammar schools to get to know one another. The links which are established through such activities persist long after membership has lapsed. By enabling young Catholics from grammar schools to get to know one another, they contribute to a network of relationships amongst the former pupils of different schools. They are undoubtedly a factor of considerable importance in establishing a sense of being 'the same sort of people'. Young Catholics learn from this contact with one another that the pupils and former pupils of other grammar schools look at matters in the same light as themselves.

Thus, while the extra-parochial groups do not appear to be important in some ways, the manner in which they enable a sense of solidarity with Catholics of a similar education to develop makes their function a crucial one in the development of the emerging section of Catholics who have been to grammar schools. Were it not for the activities of such organizations, it seems probable that many would be much less in contact with other Catholics. Whatever their stated aims, however, the function that such groups perform seems to be concerned with the cultural rather than the religious aspects of Catholicism, contributing as they do to social solidarity amongst those who have received a grammar school education in Catholic schools.

Chapter 10

FRIENDSHIP AND LEISURE

THE preceding three chapters have been concerned with groups which, in their different ways, have been formally established within the institutional framework of the Roman Catholic Church. Some, like the University Catholic Societies, are designed to fit a particular social situation, an attempt to meet a contemporary need. The social systems of the parish, on the other hand, have grown up round a legal and administrative unit in response to the demands of a variety of cultural settings, in different historical contexts. But in spite of the wide variations in legal status and social composition, the organizations so far described all form a part of the institutional life of the Catholic Church.

It remains, therefore, to consider the question of informal relationships of the former pupils of Catholic grammar schools. What did they choose to do with the time that was at their disposal for leisure—and more important—with whom did they choose to spend it? What effect did their educational experiences have upon their choice of friends? What were the criteria for selecting close friends—education, religion, occupation, social class, or some other factor? Their own descriptions of their religious attitudes and opinions have been reported. What are the social consequences of these beliefs in relation to their leisure time and, more especially, to their choice of friends?[1] How far are they now in contact with other Catholics? Some went to parochial schools; have the links established at an early age at these schools withstood the later separation in secondary schools? How far has contact, before and after leaving school, with people who do not share their religious views led to close relationships with them?

In trying to find answers to these questions, the study is in effect considering the consequences of Catholic grammar school education not only for Roman Catholicism, but also for the wider society. It is showing how a particular educational pattern is distributing a section of people in society, and how it may act as a means of social change, or how it may perpetuate attitudes and social systems already in existence.

School Friendships

The main interest of this part of the survey was, of course, centred in friendships in existence at the time of the fieldwork, but school

1. Cf. Lenski, *op. cit.*, *passim*.

friendships were also included, in the hope that this would lead to a deeper understanding of the situation. In fact, they proved very relevant to the study from two points of view. Firstly, they revealed how far present friendships had started at school, and secondly, they indicated in yet another way the great importance of the school community.

While the pupils were at school, their closest friends tended to be others who were not only at the same school, but also in the same class. A few mentioned that their patterns of friendship had altered after the Fifth Form, when one or more of their companions had left school, while they themselves continued to the Sixth Form. Usually they had then become closer to an individual or group with whom they had already been on good terms. The fact that time for out of school activities was limited undoubtedly contributed to this concentration of friendships upon the school.

Some had attended grammar schools which had a particularly small Sixth Form, or one which was divided into sections according to the type of subject taken; this often resulted in the entire group regarding one another as friends. As one reply had it:

I went round with quite a large group. The whole form was very closely knit.

But even within such groups, there were always some who were regarded as closer friends than others.

For the most part, living in the same neighbourhood did not appear to be decisive in determining friendships. There were a few who had friends living nearby while they were at school, but in general these friendships had arisen through contact at school rather than in the neighbourhood.[1] However, travelling to and from school together had in a few instances led to increased contact and also apparently to a deepening of relationships.

Although everybody included at least one special friend from the same grammar school, it must be added that there was a small proportion of respondents who had close companions outside school. Fourteen per cent mentioned people who were at different schools, including some who were not at grammar schools. There was one young man who was firm in his statement that he had no friends at all while he was at school.

All named other Catholics amongst their closest friends while they were at school; there were a handful, however, included in the answers who were not Catholics. The question on religion was often greeted with amazement when the friends were class mates. But the query was made even when people from the same school were men-

1. Cf. Fichter, *Social Relations, op. cit.*, p. 174.

tioned, to avoid making an assumption which might not have been justified—at least three of the schools used to admit non-Catholic pupils in the past. The way in which their friends' religion was described was interesting; often the religion was not termed 'Catholic', but 'the same as mine', or even, 'the same—of course'. A few looked taken aback and made a joking remark, such as, 'Catholic, of course. At least, I *hope* they still are!'

It is worth noting that, in answering this question, only one person included someone of the opposite sex. It was evident from the remarks that were made that a number of those who were interviewed had gone out with members of the opposite sex while they were still at school, but apparently only one young woman considered the relationship had been a sufficiently stable one to merit inclusion amongst special friends, a finding which would probably not be true of those in their last years at secondary modern schools.

Present Friendships

If the pattern of friendships can be described as relatively simple while respondents were still at school, this is certainly not true of the time when they were interviewed. They were asked to confine themselves to those they usually went around with, but even so it was most difficult to extract meaningful information from the immense variety of relationships which were reported.

Only 2 per cent were married, but 31 per cent were either engaged or courting. A few of these had little contact with other friends. One young man explained, for instance, 'I'm engaged now. I see a lot of the girlfriend.' Another answered the question even more briefly by saying, 'My girl'. Several young men whose former class mates were now engaged or courting complained that once they had become involved in a steady relationship of this sort, contact with them ceased, because girlfriends expected leisure time to be spent with them.

Apart from those who were courting, 27 per cent mentioned a special friend of the same sex with whom they spent a large amount of their leisure time. However, some of these belonged to groups as well; 40 per cent referred to belonging to a group, and another 14 per cent said they preferred to spend their time with several groups. This was sometimes the case with university students, especially those who were away from Liverpool during termtime; several of these had kept up their school friendships as well as starting new relationships away from home, as the following replies show:

I've still kept up the school friends. I've new friends at university.
I still go round with those people [i.e. those described as school friends]. They're my main female friends. There are others at university, so it's mainly during the holidays that I see them.

Nineteen per cent of the answers contained references to having several separate companions who were seen individually, rather than one special person or group.

One would expect that the extent to which people had close relationships with non-Catholics would have increased since they left school. However, it is particularly noticeable that there was only one person who did not include at least one Catholic among her closest friends. In fact, as many as 61 per cent said that all those they had named were Catholics. Occasionally it was added that a particular person was no longer a practising Catholic. The extent to which respondents had maintained or established new friendships with Catholics is all the more noticeable since the study included university students and young men who were employed in industry, people who had many opportunities to become friendly with those who did not share their religious beliefs. It must be emphasized, of course, that these questions referred only to close relationships and obviously excluded those whom respondents might have described as friends in a different context. But the fact remains that after naming their closest companions, with only one exception, all described some of those mentioned as Catholics, and well over half of those who were interviewed reported that all their close friends were Catholics.

It was interesting to see how many again identified themselves with Catholicism in describing religion. The phrase 'the same as mine' was used once more, but there was another form of description which revealed how respondents allied themselves to the in-group; those who were not Catholics were rarely given the name of their religion. They were usually termed 'non-Catholic'. Occasionally this was followed by an explanation, such as 'She's a Methodist', but sometimes they did not even know their friends' religion. The important framework for them was Catholicism, and they defined religion according to membership of the group with which they identified themselves.

One of the most significant points about friendship was that not only were many of the close companions of those who were interviewed Catholics, they were Catholics of a similar educational background. As many as 67 per cent were still in close contact with class mates from the same Catholic grammar schools as themselves. The following excerpts illustrate the way in which many had kept in touch with school fellows:

I go round with the same girl [i.e. the one mentioned in response to the question on school friends] and the others [from school] while they're at home.

More or less the same people—the friends from school days.

This closeness of contact with other Catholics who had received a grammar school education is highlighted by the additional fact that the former pupils of other Catholic grammar schools in the area were included in as many as 31 per cent of the answers. It was rare for someone to mention that those they were friendly with had been educated at secondary modern schools, on the one hand, or at public schools, on the other, Catholic or otherwise. As few as 2 per cent reported that they had friends whose last school had been a parochial one. Education was apparently a very important factor in influencing the choice of close companions. It seems that their education and the social experiences to which it had led them made these young people feel at ease only in the company to which they had grown accustomed through school.

The close contact with school fellows was further confirmed by the remarks made when people described the ways in which they saw their former class mates from grammar schools. Although some made special arrangements to keep in touch with these people, it seems that most had no need to do this. Those who were at the University of Liverpool, for instance, saw fellow students who had been in the same form at school regularly without having to make any efforts to keep in touch. Others knew that there were places where they were sure to meet acquaintances with whom they had been friendly at school. Plainly they were familiar with one another's habits in this respect.

Just over half had friends whose occupations were the same as their own. Another 27 per cent said that while one or more of the people they had mentioned shared their occupations, some of their friends had jobs of a different type. This was particularly true of companions of the opposite sex, as one would expect. Several young men who were or had been students had girlfriends whose occupations were lower in the social scale than their own.

Sometimes meetings were arranged at the places where respondents worked or studied. Others were accustomed to meet at one another's homes, or preferred to make arrangements every time. Special meeting places were also mentioned, including the Reference Library, because many students studied there during university vacations.

Another type of rendezvous mentioned by young men was a public house. It is worth noting that in addition to those which had become the meeting place of a group, there were two where casual encounters between school fellows were frequent. One of these was situated near one of the schools; and more important, the premises of the Old Boys' Association was opposite the school, so this pub acted as a popular meeting place. The former pupils of other Catholic grammar schools also used it frequently, for many were associate members of the organization in question. The other was in the centre of the city, and was owned in fact by a former pupil of one of the schools. It was clear during visits with former pupils of boys' Catholic grammar schools that one of the functions of this place was to act as a meeting place for the 'old boys' of at least two of the schools in the survey. It was interesting to see at the weekends that if the 'regulars' missed the people they wanted to meet, they could often locate them in another pub frequented by the group.

Leisure Time Interests

The question of leisure time interests at school sometimes evoked answers such as 'homework', or 'Leisure time? I didn't have any!' Although all did in fact go on to describe activities which they had enjoyed while they were at school, it appeared that most had taken their studies seriously and had little time to spare. The most popular activity, especially with the boys, was sport, and this was often associated with the school, highlighting yet again the focus on the school community. The following examples illustrate how sport dominated the free time of many while they were at school:

Rugby. Cricket. Tennis. Swimming. Mainly sporting interests. For a time I was keen on cycling.
Sport. That was just about it. The cinema and some reading.

Reading was an important leisure time activity; music, too, figured often in the answers. Dancing was also popular, but not to the extent to which it was after leaving school. Most ex-pupils seemed to have maintained the interests which they had at school, adding to rather than changing them. Sport was less prominent in the girls' answers than it had been when they described their school interests. Clearly time continued to be an important consideration for those who were still studying. The following excerpts illustrate the way in which the question on leisure time activities was answered:

Much the same. I play a lot of sport. I still read and the cinema is my chief entertainment.
Jazz. Football. Occasionally I watch television. And reading.
I like dancing. I don't do a lot of reading. I go walking a lot.

A good deal of free time appeared to be spent informally with friends, often at one another's houses. In fact, this was probably the most popular way of spending one's leisure. Respondents found it hard to describe this sort of behaviour; one young man, for instance, whose later replies revealed a very active social life, answered, 'I haven't any. If I go out at weekends, I go to coffee bars and pubs with friends.' There were numerous comments again about a dislike for organizations, and this was attributed by some to an anti-social nature. The stereotype is revealed in the following answer, given by a young man who had just got his degree:

I go dancing and to the pictures. Or I just go for a drink. I'm too much of a lone wolf to go into organizations. I had the parish priest round a few weeks ago to ask me to be the scoutmaster . . . I also got a leaflet from another Catholic organization . . . It's a good idea if you like that sort of thing. *I* can't stand it.

It would, however, be extremely misleading to view this attitude apart from the behaviour of the people concerned. Although they frequently stressed their dislike of organized groups, they seemed to live very full social lives, the emphasis being always on informality. This explains the popularity amongst the former pupils of the boys' schools of casual visits to places such as a public house where one could be sure of meeting friends; in this way they were free of any obligation to attend if they did not feel inclined to do so. Although the patterns of friendship among the girls were rather different, since they tended to have a particular friend or group of friends whom they met regularly, the emphasis was still on informality, an attitude which makes the lack of interest in parochial and other organizations all the more comprehensible.

Contact with Fellow Pupils of Primary Schools

In considering contacts with former class mates from primary schools, it was interesting to see that there was a broad distinction between the ex-pupils of parochial schools and those of private preparatory schools. Many of the class mates of the latter had accompanied them to grammar schools and had maintained their connections after school life had come to an end. Even when such acquaintances had later attended different grammar schools, it seems that there was still a greater likelihood of coming into contact with them. They were often met at social functions, such as a dance held by a Catholic association, perhaps the Catholic Colleges' Ball, or at a Catholic training college, or at university. Although such people might not have attended the same grammar school, they tended to receive a similar level of education, and so come into contact later. They were regarded as belonging to the in-group and were 'placed' in it by one another.

This was very different from the situation of those who had attended parochial junior schools, an important finding. Most of these had lost contact with their previous class mates. A few were still in regular contact with them, but it must be stressed that they were not typical; they were a handful whose leisure time was largely spent in

the neighbourhood, perhaps in parish activities. The following replies came from two young men who had attended the parish school;
they were both university students:

Oh, yes, every night—I go with them.
Oh, yes, most of them are in the Catholic Young Men's Society in the
parish and play football for the C.Y.M.S.

But although most of those who had attended parochial schools reported that they had 'seen' in the literal sense their former class
mates, this did not necessarily involve social contact. The following
excerpts, repeated in many answers, give some indication of the level
of contact experienced by the majority of those who had attended
parochial schools:

I see them around and acknowledge them in the street and at church.
I suppose I do when I go to church, but I'm completely out of touch. We
don't recognize one another.
I see them because I still live in the same district, but we've lost social
contact. We still say, 'Hello'. I see them in the street and coming out of
church.

Seeing former class mates in these ways was mentioned frequently
by those who had gone to parochial schools. But it seems that social
distances had widened with the separation in school. Previous class
mates were now moving in a different circle. Their occupations were
of a lower status, and their leisure time interests differed. Education,
it seems, has effectively introduced divisions between former class
mates, and through the attitudes and ideas it has communicated to
some *via* the grammar schools, it has altered a section of society.

Conclusions

One of the most striking findings of the survey is the extent to which
close friends tended not only to be Catholics, but to be Catholics who
had either been fellow pupils, or had attended another Catholic
grammar school in the same neighbourhood. This contact was
fostered by the activities which had grown up round the schools,
such as dances organized by former pupils' associations. Such activities enabled young Catholics from grammar schools to get to know
one another, and the friendships remained after interest had been
lost in formal activities. It was clear, too, that not only did this encourage friendships, but also it sharpened their awareness of the
existence of other Catholics of similar education, and strengthened
the mutual knowledge of each other. This was true even in the absence of personal acquaintance. Thus, the activities of these organizations, although they were rejected by many at a later stage, seem to

perform an important function from the cultural point of view; through the contact they provide at an early age, they facilitate the growth of awareness of other Catholics of similar educational experiences. Feelings of solidarity can ripen in such a setting, and manifest themselves in phenomena such as that of 'placing' one another in the in-group.

At the same time, contact with fellow pupils from the parochial schools was reduced to a minimum. Respondents shared their religious beliefs with them, but in ordinary social situations they did not identify themselves with former class mates, seeing themselves as different sorts of Catholics. These attitudes of discrimination on the basis of education were also revealed in describing reactions to parochial activities. Education, it seems, has produced new attitudes which are stronger in some contexts than localized religious loyalties.

Thus grammar school education has not resulted in the breakdown of relationships between Catholics, but rather a rearrangement of them. Social divisions have been created between former class mates at parochial schools. Subsequent education has drawn them apart, removing those who went to grammar schools into another section of society. It seems that the sharing of religious beliefs is in itself not enough to create a bond between individuals as far as ordinary social relationships are concerned, and this represents one of the most important findings of the investigation.

As Fichter points out in describing the American scene,[1] educated Catholics tend to identify more easily with non-Catholics of a similar education than with their fellow Catholics who remain at the parochial school. The consequences of this for the social organization of Catholicism are likely to be even more far-reaching in the future. The results described so far in this book have indicated that educated Catholics are being lost to the parish, by and large. If this trend continues, as there seems every likelihood that it will, parochial activities will suffer even more. In viewing this finding, it is as well to stop to consider if perhaps in the long run, a concept of the Church which is able to detach itself from a particular social organization, designed for the needs of Catholics in a particular historical context, may not be of more value, not only to individual Catholics but to the Church as a whole.

Apart from the consequences for the parochial structure, this trend towards identification with those of the same social class has even wider implications. The former pupils of Catholic grammar schools already show acceptance of many of the cultural values trans-

---

1. 'Modal parishioners, whether they have graduated from Catholic or secular universities, identify more closely with non-Catholic college graduates than they do with fellow-parishioners of less education', *op. cit.*, p. 50.

mitted through the educational system.[1] But while education has created social divisions between former class mates, it cannot be said that a *diaspora* has occurred amongst Catholics, for the former pupils of Catholic grammar schools remain in many ways members of tightly knit communities. True, these are informal, as they are based on friendship, but the close ties within them show that they still bear many of the characteristics of the early communities of Liverpool Catholics. Defensive attitudes towards the wider community, for example, still tend to be one of their outstanding characteristics. To give one another support, their members remain in close contact. Although their friendships are not restricted to Catholics, the closest tend to be based on a sharing of religious beliefs and education. So while those concerned have rejected the formal groupings of Catholicism, their educational experiences have introduced them to a strong network of relationships.

They have identified themselves not simply with the emerging middle class but rather with a section within it, a section defined according to its education and religion. Instead of being completely assimilated into the middle class, they have developed their own sub-group within it. In this way, a new cultural form of Roman Catholicism is developing in Liverpool. It still remains, however, to discover how long this network of relationships between former pupils of Catholic grammar schools lasts. What happens when they marry, and some move away? There is evidence to suggest that at least some of the features which characterize those who have recently left school are to be found in an older section of the ex-pupils of Catholic grammar schools in Liverpool. Although the contact between former class mates may not be so close, there are nevertheless indications that feelings of familiarity and solidarity with other former pupils of Catholic grammar schools still persist.

   1. The relationship between cultural and religious values needs to be considered more deeply. Such an analysis would again approach ideas developed by Weber in his study of the consequences of the Protestant ethic, *The Protestant Ethic and the Spirit of Capitalism*, New York, 1930. Reprinted 1950.

Chapter 11

ST. HENRY'S: A PAROCHIAL SURVEY

IT was plain from the evidence collected in the course of this investigation that a fundamental lack of interest in the parish was general amongst the former pupils of Catholic grammar schools in Liverpool, and that they were often reluctant to take part in its social activities. The question must now be considered, however, how far the attitudes of these people are similar to those of young Catholics who had not attended grammar schools.

It could be argued that this happens with all young Catholics in Liverpool. Some evidence to the contrary has, however, already been presented in discussing the views of the parish priests, who often considered that their parishioners who had attended the parochial schools remained steadfast in their allegiance to the parish, even though this might not lead to active participation. It seemed, therefore, that additional fieldwork would be useful to discover more about this problem. When the interviews with the headteachers, the survey among the former pupils of grammar schools, and the views of the parish priests had all been carefully examined, it was decided that the question should be tackled from another point of view altogether. A single parish was selected for study, and parochial groups in it were subjected to analysis according to the education of their members. At the same time, it was hoped to discover how the parishioners regarded those who went to grammar schools, and how they evaluated their behaviour.

After visiting many parochial groups in several parishes, a parish was eventually selected for study, which will be known in this account as 'St. Henry's'.[1] This contained various useful features. It was large and suburban, and comprised two main types of housing, both local authority estates and a considerable amount of privately owned property. It had its own school, which was divided into two parts; the primary school was next to the church in the old tradition. The parishioners were extremely proud of the primary school's consistent degree of success in getting pupils to grammar schools, so there was no danger that the number of parishioners with a grammar school education would be small.

1. The evidence which is relevant to the main inquiry is presented briefly in this chapter. It is hoped to give more attention to other aspects of the findings in St. Henry's parish elsewhere at a later date.

Another advantage was that there were numerous groups for young people in the parish. But the greatest advantage was probably the fact that the clergy were willing to co-operate; in particular, one of the curates gave a great deal of assistance. The active parishioners, too, were most helpful.

St. Henry's Senior School

St. Henry's senior school was visited on a number of occasions, and the headmaster was interviewed twice. The investigator also met other members of the staff. Tremendous pride was taken in the school by both teachers and clergy which revealed itself in many ways, such as in describing the school's successes in sports matches with other schools. Another subject which aroused great enthusiasm in all the parochial schools visited during all the fieldwork was the way in which each of them had been built; the interviewer was always given details of how the various sections had been added to them, and how other parts had been altered. It was particularly noticeable that the headmaster and the teachers at St. Henry's senior school were proud of their pupils, and resented the attitude which dismissed such children as 'grammar school failures'. Although the school was a large one, the headmaster, who had been there for many years, prided himself on knowing all his pupils and their family background intimately, and it seemed that this was not an idle boast; parishioners who had been educated in the school spoke highly of him and remembered him with affection.

Education of Active Parishioners

As the membership registers of parochial associations did not include the educational history of the members, information had to be sought elsewhere. In the smaller associations this was not difficult, as members could be asked for this personally. In the larger organizations, however, the particulars had to be obtained from the officers, which was a less reliable procedure. The interviewer attended several meetings of all the groups in the parish where it was possible to do so unobtrusively. In view of the general slant of this research, particular attention was given to the organizations catering for younger parishioners. It proved surprisingly easy to take part in most of the meetings. In fact, the interviewer was often greeted as a prospective member and invited to join. The idea of using this role, at least by implication, was discarded on the grounds that it was both too limiting and introduced too many complications into the situation. The interviewer was continually amazed at the ease with which the explanation 'She's doing some research', was accepted. An asset in gaining acceptance was that the interviewer had already familiarized herself with most of the groups elsewhere, and knew therefore what was expected of her at the meetings.

Although the findings from one or two of the organizations catering for older parishioners tended to be rather inconclusive because reliable information was difficult to collect, certain patterns were discerned in the membership of younger groups in the parish. What emerges most clearly from the findings is the central influence of St. Henry's school upon membership of parochial organizations. In the Guild of St. Agnes, for instance, catering for girls aged between eight and fifteen, there was only a handful of members, out of over seventy on the register, who did not attend St. Henry's school. The leader of the group, who had herself attended a grammar school, was of the opinion that those who went to grammar schools dropped their membership because they 'felt out of it'. She commented:

I think at first they think they're too good. Afterwards they have homework. They feel a bit shy when there's only one of them.

It was, in fact, noticeable at the meetings attended by the interviewer that the one or two children present from grammar schools were conspicuous amongst the others because of their school uniforms, and also because they seemed shy in approaching the other children.[1]

At the age of fifteen, the members of the Guild were supposed to transfer to the Children of Mary, one of the traditional groups in the parish, consisting of women only. Here, too, it was noticeable that nearly all the members had attended St. Henry's school. Plainly, most of them had known one another from childhood, and those to whom the interviewer talked were emphatic in their statements that they would not have come to the meetings if they had not expected to find other people there whom they knew. The grammar school girls, in general, they said, would not know anyone. One of the younger parishioners who had been to a local grammar school, now in another organization in the parish, described how she had felt isolated when she had gone to a Children of Mary meeting for the first and only time:

I went to a grammar school. I didn't know anyone from the parish. I kept myself to myself! The priest got me to go to the Children of Mary. I went one evening into the hall. I didn't know them . . . The people at school [i.e. the parochial school] with me weren't there. They're scattered.

It appeared that recruitment for the Guild and the Children of Mary was carried out through the parochial school; the younger

1. The interviewer checked with the leader that no other grammar school children were present, in case they were indistinguishable from the rest.

girls were constantly encouraged to join the Guild, and the priest invited those who were ready to leave school to attend the meetings of the Children of Mary. Thus, the area of recruitment was largely confined to those who went to St. Henry's school. Members of the Children of Mary and the priests encouraged others whom they knew to come, but it seemed that those who went to grammar schools had usually lost touch with their former class mates.

The Boys' Club, disbanded at the time of the fieldwork because, in the words of one of the curates, 'it was best known for being broken up every couple of weeks', had also consisted largely of boys attending St. Henry's school.

With the teams of the Young Christian Workers, too, the influence of the parochial school made itself felt.[1] The groups for girls of school age, or the 'Pre -Y.C.W.', as they were known, met in the school itself, although it was officially a parochial organization, not one attached to the school. One section consisted entirely of girls at St. Henry's school, and the other group had only two members who attended grammar schools; both of these girls had maintained friendships with class mates from the primary school.

In the teams of the Y.C.W. whose members were actually working, there were several members who had also attended grammar schools, especially in the Leaders' Team. What was particularly noticeable, however, was that nearly all those who had gone to grammar schools had first passed through St. Henry's primary school. They had either maintained or re-established relationships with their earlier class mates. It was evident, however, that most of those who had gone to grammar schools had lost all social contact with former fellow pupils in the parochial school.[2] The leaders of the boys' team, for instance, were of the opinion that grammar school parishioners were uninterested in parochial meetings. Like the groups already described, they depended largely upon the parochial school for recruiting members, and those who attended grammar schools were contacted only through the informal system of 'lads knowing other lads'.

Among the organizations for older parishioners, there were two, the St. Vincent de Paul Society and the Legion of Mary, which had a noticeable proportion of members educated in grammar schools (approximately one-fifth and one-third respectively). These groups, however, were significantly different from the other associations in their methods of recruitment. Both recruited selectively, and membership obligations were strictly observed.

1. Cf. A. Smith, *The Young Christian Worker Movement and the Influence of the Social Milieu on Religion*, unpublished manuscript, cited with permission.
2. Cf. Ward, *op. cit.*, p. 97.

Influence of the Family

In general, it was noticeable in St. Henry's parish that, as in St. Catherine's parish, the influence of the family was of vast importance.[1] Parents introduced their children to membership of parochial organizations, and it was striking that almost all the former pupils of grammar schools who were members of organizations in St. Henry's parish either belonged to families which were active or else had maintained or re-established earlier friendships from the parochial school. The findings of this part of the fieldwork, then, confirm those of the main survey: for a handful of those who go to grammar schools, the influence of family and friends is more important than attitudes and patterns of behaviour learned at school. In the majority of cases, however, the school was a more important influence in producing attitudes towards the parish.

Influence of the Parochial School

Something has already been seen of the influence of the parochial school upon membership of parochial organizations. The area of recruitment for several organizations was largely confined to those who attended St. Henry's school, and other factors, such as two of the groups meeting in the school itself, helped to identify the school and the parish even further.

While the findings permit only tentative conclusions, it seems worthwhile putting forward other points relevant in this context. Although it seems that the parochial school had succeeded in making the pupils conscious of the parish as an important social institution in their lives, their concept of the parish seemed at times to have little reference at all to religion. For instance, the results of a questionnaire administered by one of the curates to the girls in their last year at school, sixteen of them, showed that nearly all demanded a mixed youth club and dance in the parish. The replies, and subsequent talks the interviewer had on a number of occasions with the school leavers from St. Henry's, showed various interesting distinctions between the attitudes of these young people and the outlook of pupils and ex-pupils of grammar schools. The answers of the girls at St. Henry's indicated how often they identified the school with the parish; for instance, one girl had this to say:

I think a very interesting thing which would keep us off the streets at night would be to have a mixed youth club in the parish, because I think that the boys of this school are much better provided for, in, for example, the Boys' Club.

1. Ward, *op cit.*, p.. 116.

It was the social side of the parish which was most real to those who went to St. Henry's schools, in sharp distinction to the lack of interest shown towards this aspect by those who had been to grammar schools. The demands for a youth club, which was a burning question in St. Henry's parish at the time of the fieldwork (the parish priest being adamant in his refusal to allow one), revealed plainly how the parish was accepted as a source of social activities; a youth club was wanted, and it was to the parish that these young people looked for it. In their conversation, too, they showed their identification with the parish, speaking in terms of '*We* should have this . . .' They had learned to expect that the parish should perform certain functions for them, although they were not always too clear as to what these were. The religious aspects of the parish were often explicitly rejected, and the religious associations were dismissed as 'pious'; one girl, for instance, made the following complaint:

We would like a mixed youth club which would not be so religious, as we are always getting told about our religion, and sometimes you get sick of it and wish you weren't born a Catholic.

It was plain that these young people who were still at school saw life in terms of the neighbourhood in which they lived. One of their favourite recreations was 'hanging round'. Due to the nature of the district, such groups of teenagers were not so noticeable as they are in central areas of Liverpool, at street corners and the like, but there were certain meeting places in St. Henry's parish which fulfilled the same function for these young people as the more obvious rendezvous in the centre of the city.

Views of the Clergy and Active Parishioners

The parish priest of St. Henry's had already been interviewed earlier in this investigation, and he had spontaneously expressed his disappointment at the reactions of grammar school parishioners towards the parish. He was firmly convinced that a Catholic's first responsibility was to his parish; all extra-parochial loyalties should take second place. He considered, too, that the grammar schools were failing to produce leaders of parochial life. The former pupils ought, in his view, to be willing to take on more responsibilities than the ordinary parishioners; their educational privileges gave them this duty. He had made considerable efforts ever since he came to the parish to draw these people into parochial life, but his appeals had met with no response. The curates, too, found it difficult to attract grammar school parishioners to parochial associations.

The pastor was also indignant at the manner in which those who had received a grammar school education viewed his authority. He found them critically disposed towards his suggestions, and he considered their demands for explanations of his actions in the parish were inappropriate to their role as parishioners. In his eyes, they lacked the respect for the priest's authority which should characterize the relationship between pastor and laity. It can be seen that this traditional view frequently met with opposition from the former pupils of grammar schools.

Active parishioners, too, it seems, thought that such people were reluctant to take part in parochial activities; the officers of organizations found them difficult to contact, unless another member of the family or a friend brought them along to meetings. Some seemed to accept with resignation the fact that these people had gone from the parish, almost as if it were part of the order of things. 'They have homework', it was said, or 'they have no time'. Sometimes, too, parishioners suggested such people were 'snobbish', but not so often as it might have been expected. However they evaluated the situation, they obviously did not expect Catholics who went to grammar schools to share their own interest in the parish. The very fact of going to grammar schools seemed to remove these people from the parish in the opinion of some. Ties of friendship and familiarity which might have developed at the parochial school seemed to have been dropped when some left to go to grammar schools. Thus, not only did the customary method of recruiting miss grammar school pupils, but it seems that they were regarded as a separate section of people by the other parishioners and were not expected to fit into the traditional ways of behaving.

Conclusions

These findings are relevant to the present study only in so far as they throw light upon the major issue which is being considered, that is to say, the consequences of grammar school education for the social organizatior of Roman Catholicism. It seems that active parishioners in St. Henry's parish, as well as the clergy, regarded those who went to grammar schools as having a different outlook from themselves. Education has apparently tended to alter the relationships between parishioners as well as between clergy and laity.

The differences which exist in outlook can be seen to some extent when the ideas of the pupils and former pupils of St. Henry's school are compared with those of the former pupils of grammar schools. The pupils at St. Henry's were educated to think of the parish as important to their lives; they had learned to live in a local community, and their ties to the neighbourhood were strong at this stage. In the grammar schools, on the other hand, territorial boundaries receded into the background. In class the pupils made friends from all over the city, and even further afield, and these ties of friendship were more powerful in influencing the majority of them than links with their homes and neighbourhood.

As a result of their education, St. Henry's pupils looked to the parish as a means of social interaction; as Chapter 7 has shown, it was this aspect of the parish which was least acceptable to those who went to grammar schools. The latter acknowledged that the parish might fulfil this function for some people, but they hastened to add that they did not identify themselves with Catholics who were interested in the parish. St. Henry's young people, on the other hand, wanted the parish to offer them more facilities for a social community, one without religious connotations, they sometimes added. They criticized the parish for failing to live up to their expectations because their interest was a personal one. The ex-pupils of grammar schools looked at the parish in a more detached manner, and suggested activities for other people, usually making it plain that they themselves would not be interested. They were insistent that they had no time for organized activities, while those at the parochial school, and some active parishioners who had also been to St. Henry's school, complained that there were not enough groups in existence. Here,then, are two fundamentally different approaches to the parish.

It appears from the results of this investigation that part of the Catholic educational system in Liverpool is transmitting traditional cultural values and ideas about Catholicism, while the other part is communicating a new approach, and new attitudes towards the social systems of the Catholic Church. Both traditional and changing ideas are, however, expected to live amicably side by side in the old social context. They do not appear to be succeeding in this; the former pupils of grammar schools seem to have been removed, by and large, from the parochial system. Only a few adjust to the traditional way of living, through loyalty to their families and former class mates. A basic sense of irrelevance and lack of interest prevents the majority from belonging to the parish as a social community.

Emphasis has been placed in this research upon the consequences of grammar school education; but the changes being brought about in the social organization of Catholicism now need to be tackled from another angle, from the point of view of the greater numbers attending secondary modern schools. The all-age parochial school has had its day; the inter-parochial school, serving several parishes, is becoming increasingly expedient, and it is likely to have radical consequences for the parish. By considering what is happening as a result of these other educational innovations, further light might be thrown upon the ways in which changes are introduced into religious values and institutions. In such an analysis it should also be possible to discover how far later experiences, such as marriage, either maintain or break down the cultural barriers which have developed as a result of the educational system.

Chapter 12

CONCLUSIONS

THE breakdown of traditional institutions is but one indication of the rapid changes in ideas and attitudes which are taking place in the world today. In spite of their relevance to social policies of all kinds, we know as yet remarkably little about how these developments are brought about and even less about their consequences for the individuals and groups who experience them. In particular, there are few studies which trace the relationships between institutions established in society for different purposes. Recent surveys examining the consequences of educational innovations for the class structure represent the growing awareness that we need to examine a social institution against the background of other groups and social structures which are related to it at any one point.

By considering the ways in which education has affected the organization of a religious body and the relationships within it, through altering the social class of some of its members, this investigation has tried to discover a little about how changes may be introduced into traditional contexts. Many social policies have had unexpected, even disastrous, consequences for individuals and whole sections of society precisely because social institutions and relationships do not react upon one another in a manner which is either direct or readily perceived. The numerous ways in which values and attitudes can affect social relationships offer, therefore, a particularly important field for research.

This survey of religious institutions and behaviour was carried out against a background of one of the most exciting periods in history. Changes in attitudes towards religious groups and structures are taking place so rapidly that it is difficult to carry out an analysis which is sufficiently dynamic. It has been these swift developments in social life throughout the world which have led to the formal acknowledgement in the Roman Catholic Church, through the convening of the Vatican Council in 1962, that such changes may produce new needs which cannot always be met by adaptations on the part of traditional structures suited to earlier generations and different historical contexts. The separation of whole classes of the population from the Church at various times indicates to some extent the consequences of insufficient attention to changes in social conditions.

There is, too, a growing awareness that there are many discussions with regard to the religious life today which cannot be settled exclusively by reference to scriptural or theological authorities; a comprehensive examination of such issues requires factual information about current behaviour and attitudes. For Christianity is not a set of beliefs and ideas which exist in the spiritual sphere alone, but a way of life involving the commitment of the whole person. The social institutions of the environment in which the Christian lives are not, therefore, alien or profane, but a part of the natural order to be used in God's redemptive plans. And at the same time, the beliefs must express themselves in social living and need institutions to develop and support them. Hence the tremendous importance for the religious life of understanding all the social institutions and patterns of behaviour in a particular *milieu*, and especially of the interaction of the religious and other institutions. It is necessary to discover how far social structures designed to incorporate Christian beliefs are still able to do so, and how far they are meaningful at the present time.

It has been the aim of the present study to discover how far values and beliefs persist through education and to what extent traditional structures continue to express them. So far this book has outlined some of the consequences which an educational policy has had not only for the individuals whose lives it has altered, but also for the social organization of the religious group to which they belong. It remains now to discuss how far these findings throw light upon the wider issues which were examined in the first chapter.

Changes in Social Structures

The investigation was concerned with the effect in the religious sphere of a deliberate plan to alter the educational system, a plan which has resulted in new patterns of social mobility. The gradual disappearance of the social homogeneity of Roman Catholicism in Liverpool has been sharply accelerated in recent years. The sons and daughters of working-class families now attend universities in increasing numbers. A single family may experience in a few years changes which were previously accomplished over several generations. What consequences have these changes in the social structure of Catholicism had for the social organization of the Church? How far has a uniform social grouping, centred on the parish, persisted in spite of changes in the class system? What has been the overall effect on the religious and social life of those who have borne the brunt of these changes?

It can be seen that the educational system has operated as an agent of change in that it has given similar experiences to young people of widely differing social class, and has thus made them conscious of having a great deal in common with one another. For many from working-class homes, the ideas and ways of behaving they learn in the grammar schools from their teachers and school fellows become more important and more real than those of their families. The findings of this study indicate how acceptable most of these young people found the focus on the school community, and the extent to which their social relationships, both as pupils and later in life, were influenced by it.

The old devotion and loyalty to the parochial settings have come to have little meaning to most of these young people who have attended grammar schools. Although allegiance to their families and former class mates still holds a few in parochial communities, the majority feel themselves removed from the old context, but not in the sense of being uprooted; on the contrary, they have shed the old ties in the parish with ease. Grammar school education has led the former pupils to regard the parish as part of a cultural way of living in which they themselves have no part. This is because their concept of the Church is more abstract than that accepted by previous generations of Catholics in the city, and their identification with Catholicism goes beyond the local setting; the parish is no longer the all-important centre of their religious lives. Their education, and the experiences which this has either given them or led them towards, have removed them into a social sphere which is unrelated to the neighbourhood. They acknowledge the value of the parish as a means of social interaction for others, but they do not see themselves as 'that sort of person'. For themselves, they demand from the parish little more than the adequate provision of religious services.

The findings of this research reveal the inability of the parochial structure, as it is currently understood by clergy and people in Liverpool, to absorb the impact of new attitudes and ideas. The parish has assimilated many changes in an urban setting, but the latest has proved beyond its powers, perhaps because it has been confronted here, not with individual desires, but with a fundamental reconstructing of the institutional framework which is associated with the increase in grammar school education. The ideas and attitudes which established the social life of the parish in the past, and adapted and sustained its organization in an urban environment, have little place in the lives of the former pupils of grammar schools. They do not even see the parish as something against which to react, but as something which is simply irrelevant, of limited importance. Even their criticisms of the parochial clergy, for instance, explosive though they may be at times, contain none of the calculated bitterness which can characterize intellectuals on the Continent of Europe. An individual priest might annoy them with his conservative approach, certain aspects of his role in the parish might be considered ill adapted to contemporary circumstances, but for the priesthood itself, respect is retained. However, in a parochial setting, the former pupils of grammar schools are simply not at ease, and they acknowledge this lack of familiarity and interest willingly, without any sense of obligation or shame.

With the extension of grammar school education, the social systems which have developed round the schools have grown in strength. It is these and not the parish which play the most important part in the lives of the pupils. The increasing emphasis upon the school, and the ways it is taking on more and more of the functions of the parish, have brought about a situation in which it has come to rival the traditional institution. It is hardly surprising, therefore, that the former pupils do not want to fit into the parish, an institution which many among them may never have really experienced or appreciated. In any case, it can be argued that the schools and organizations encountered later at universities and colleges, are better able to meet the spiritual and social needs of pupils and students than the parochial structure as it now exists.

But the continued emphasis which is placed upon the parish both legally, and in the formal policies of the Church in regions such as Liverpool, means that the attitudes and behaviour of those who have been to Catholic grammar schools may often be viewed with disapproval, especially by pastors. The results of this inquiry show how strongly some of the parish priests lamented the reluctance of the former pupils of grammar schools to take an active part in the parish; and such priests felt that in this way the institution of the grammar school has failed to fulfil one of its major functions, one which the teachers often do not consider to be their task at all. It is not surprising, therefore, that the parish priests regard education in grammar schools with mixed feelings. Further research, examining the factors involved more precisely than has been possible in this preliminary investigation, should reveal how far these attitudes are related to education in non-parochial schools, and how far they are directed towards the consequences of higher education itself. The pastors are glad at their parishioners' success, but grieve because experience has taught them that in this step some of the children are 'lost' to their care. To some priests, these young Catholics represent the Christian parable of the talents in reverse—they are seen as being like the man who received the most, yet wasted them instead of using them to the full. However one may evaluate the situation, it seems that, by and large, the educated section of parishioners are, in fact, being 'lost' to the parish at the present time.

Changes in Social Relationships

At the same time as the structural changes are taking place, new values and ways of looking at the Church and the world are communicated through the schools, which result in different relationships within the Catholic community. The most noticeable change is that which has occurred in the role system between pastor and parishioner. The roles which tradition regulated so carefully have been disturbed by changing attitudes and behaviour on the part of the laity. Some priests may still tend to expect from these new kinds of parishioners the approach and behaviour to which tradition has accustomed them. But the former pupils of grammar schools have not learned to think or behave in the ways transmitted through the parochial schools. Although some have previously attended such schools, it is the later experiences in the grammar schools which make the greater impact. Familiar with the approach of specialist non-parochial clergy, perhaps at the university, the demands of the parish priest often appear authoritarian to these young people. The pastor's advice is not sought because he is not expected to know how to cope with their problems. The parish priest, on the other hand, has grown accustomed to the fact that as far as his parishioners are concerned, the responsibility for taking the initiative lies with him. He is now confronted with lay people who seem to him argumentative and disrespectful, who criticize the way the services are conducted, or deplore the fact that he may find Bingo the only way of meeting the enormous debt he has incurred on the parish school.

The confusion which has arisen between pastor and parishioners is perhaps one of the most striking facts which this inquiry has brought to light. It is highly probable that some reading this would feel angry at the attitude of these young Catholics, and others would criticize the parish priests' approach as outdated. But the purpose of this research was not to show how far one set of people or another was at fault, but to discover the crises and tensions, as well as the hopes and enthusiasms, which surround a new development in the religious life. This situation between pastor and parishioner has not arisen out of individual ill will or indifference, but because a whole institutional framework and the relationships within it have been disturbed by changes in the wider social structure. The earlier familiarity has disappeared, and people are unaware of what to expect from one another.

Adaptation to the changing concepts of role behaviour between priests and people is unlikely to be a simple process. It does not only represent problems with regard to the pastor's responsibility and authority, for it also involves at the present time complicated atti-

tudes on the part of the laity. It can be observed that many young
Catholics, ready to voice criticisms amongst themselves about the
attitudes of parochial clergy, find it so difficult to discover a new relationship which is satisfactory to both sides that, on the rare occasions when they encounter their pastors, they tend to accept the
traditional relationship as the only possible one; the comments of
university students upon such situations reveal how often they des-
pise themselves for doing so afterwards. Thus, when they would most
like to be articulate in communicating their views, they may find
themselves unable to do so. As a result, the situation may appear at
times to remain unchanged, yet underneath new attitudes are developing towards the clergy.

It would seem, therefore, that one of the major pastoral problems
in this country is not, as in many Continental countries, to understand the ideas and behaviour of the working classes, for the background and experiences of the parochial clergy already assures this
sympathy; nor yet to come to grips with the emerging 'intellectuals',
for specialist clergy of similar education and views already exist. It is
the rapidly expanding sections of the population which fall between
the two which are likely to produce the biggest pastoral difficulties in
the next few years, and it is these which are least well provided for in
the institutional life of the Church. For their ways of thinking and
behaving fall into neither of the two categories already described;
the failure of schemes in provincial University Catholic Societies
modelled upon traditional Oxbridge patterns indicates that young
people who are emerging into the middle classes as a result of educational innovations think very differently from those whose place in the
social class hierarchy is simply maintained by university education.

The relationships between parishioners are changing, too. The investigation has described how grammar school education has divided
people who were once class mates at the parochial school, not simply
because of the time lapse, for this was overcome in the case of those
who shared a private primary education, but through social divisions.
No longer is there the same degree of social equality among parishioners as there was in earlier generations in Liverpool parishes.
'We're not the same sort', the former pupils of grammar schools say
awkwardly of themselves, sometimes ashamed of the underlying
sentiments. But they are thus acknowledging a social fact. In the
parish club, the young graduate finds he can contribute little to the
conversation, and the sad phrase, 'We have nothing to say to one
another', is heard yet again.

In extreme cases, as with some university students and graduates,
this breakdown in communication can lead to intolerance over matters such as traditional pieties and phrases, or popular art forms. At

times, criticisms of this kind fail to distinguish between superstitions, which are in themselves inimical to the development of Christian beliefs, and practices which are simply associated with the expression of Catholicism in a particular environment. Rapid changes leave some young people unable to understand that while such aspects of folk Catholicism do not help them, they may fulfil a valuable function for others who are accustomed to a different social *milieu*; for Christianity does not seek to isolate the individual from the cultural forms of the society in which he lives, but rather inspires him to develop his values in such a way that they will permeate social life and 'restore all things in Christ'.[1] Moreover, criticisms of this nature, especially with regard to aesthetic judgements, are culturally produced in precisely the same manner as the practices they are deploring.

In sum, it seems that the educational system has been instrumental in bringing about a vast amount of social change. In the first place, it has accelerated the processes of social mobility, transcending social barriers in making children from working-class families feel a part of the middle-class way of living. But at the same time, it has created new social distinctions between individuals, former class mates, even families. Religious affiliation does not seem to be a strong enough link in social situations to overcome these divisions. As far as ordinary social relationships are concerned, it seems that education in the present context is as powerful an influence as religion.[2]

Theoretical Implications of the Research

To consider again the fundamental and theoretical issues raised in Chapter 1: has this study been able to point to any relationship between values, behaviour and social institutions?

It seems that in the present situation, deliberate changes in the social institutions formed for educational purposes have led to certain values and ideas reaching a wider section of society. These, in their turn, are influencing the ways in which people behave, offering incentives to what is to them a new way of life. The attitudes which sustained the parochial community for so many years are no longer being communicated to those who are expected to accept the privileges and assume the responsibilities of higher education. Differences in attitudes and behaviour are leading to changing social relationships.

1. Epistle of St. Paul to the Ephesians, I, 10.
2. These findings can be compared with those produced by Booth at the beginning of the century, when he revealed through his analysis of religious influences in London, that it was social class which was the dominant factor in the social institutions of religious groups, Simey, *op. cit.* C.f. Lenski, *op. cit.*, *passim*.

These new ideas and ways of behaving affect the social institution of the parish, not so much through action directed towards the parish, but rather indirectly because some of the Catholic population are being removed socially from its activities. Thus, the emphasis upon the school and the structures which have grown round it have resulted in the school becoming the major frame of reference for the pupils. Through its stress upon the culture it transmits and upon its own social groups, grammar school education is having disfunctional consequences for the parish.

Not merely, then, has the social structure of Catholicism been altered by a new educational policy, but those who have been educated in grammar schools see the Church and society, and their relations to both, in a new way. Thus, the changes which are taking place in the social structure of Catholicism, as more and more young people move rapidly into the middle classes, are accompanied by their acceptance of standards and attitudes which are different from those held by earlier generations. In turn, these new attitudes and ideas are having consequences for the social organization of the Church. Whereas the parochial structure, based on the neighbourhood community, once reflected the social life of the faithful, the way of living of this growing set of people who have been to grammar schools is making itself felt in the institutional life of the Church, in their rejection, first of all, of the parochial community, and then in the development of informal groupings.

It seems, then, that a situation is occurring here which has often taken place in the history of the Church: the social life of the members is rapidly changing and is altering the formal structure and organization of the Church at the same time. Among the consequences of the increase in grammar school education has come the development of another cultural manifestation of Catholicism. The numbers of children attending grammar schools and the social systems revolving round the schools have enabled a sense of solidarity to develop in the area amongst those who have attended such schools. Although most formed no lasting attachment to any formal social grouping in the Church, they were conscious of belonging to a sub-culture of their own. Close friends were still chosen from amongst those who had shared similar educational experiences. The analysis of their friendship patterns revealed how false it would be to think of them as completely assimilated into the wider society as far as their close social relationships were concerned. These young people were conscious of belonging to a group which was socially distinct from 'parochial Catholics'. Thus, while sharing religious beliefs with other Catholics, there were times when they saw themselves as no more like some of these than they were similar to, for instance, Spanish

Catholics. Their opinions revealed how often they were similar to other members of the middle classes rather than to fellow Catholics in the working classes. While this may be due to some extent to individual contacts, it seems that the schools play an important part in this trend, through their emphasis upon the cultural values with which they have been traditionally associated. The findings, therefore, confirmed the hypothesis that the major frame of reference for such people was in fact a new cultural way of Catholicism, one produced through the educational system.

The speed with which this phenomenon has occurred in the present situation has meant that there has been no overall policy to cope with it. Old ideas are being communicated in new contexts, and *vice versa*. There are *ad hoc* schemes to meet new needs, such as the appointment of chaplains to the schools. But all these innovations have an effect upon one another. Alterations in one set of institutions have consequences for others. Problems have arisen here, between priest and parishioner, for instance, precisely because only one section of people have been affected by these particular attitudes produced through the educational system.

At the same time, it would be a mistake to think of the rest of society as remaining unchanged. Other groups are receiving new ideas from other sources, thus making the situation increasingly complex. The study in St. Henry's parish indicates that young people in parochial schools are accepting cultural ways which, while distinct from those associated with grammar school education, are also different from those of their parents. It remains for later investigations to discover what other factors are at work which may lead to changes in relationships and institutions.

The research reveals how changes which are planned may have the desired consequences, in this case the giving of opportunities to young people from a variety of social backgrounds to develop their potential ability through a particular form of schooling. It also indicates, however, that the effects of such innovations make themselves felt far beyond the sphere to which they are directed. The attitudes learned in one *milieu* and the relationships established there do not restrict themselves to this one area—especially if the changes take place in such an important sphere as the educational. This study has traced the repercussions for one set of institutions, the religious, showing how traditional structures and relationships have been fundamentally altered. It has also indicated other areas which have been affected: the ways in which patterns of friendship have been influenced by these changes, for instance. Consequences for relationships within the family, too, have been detected at times. Other areas remain to be considered. But it can at least be said at the present time that more research could profitably be directed towards the relationships between institutions established for different purposes. For social relationships and institutions do not exist in a vacuum; their changing form may have a variety of consequences, many of them unintended.

By considering the social consequences of a new educational policy, it has been possible to trace in this study some of the ways whereby the organization of a religious group may be radically altered. By deliberate innovation, the social institution of the school has been the means of introducing values and attitudes to a wider context. These ideas and attitudes have led to new patterns of behaviour which in their turn have been instrumental in altering traditional structures. By attempting to cope with the observable consequences of social change, religious policies and institutions have contributed to the direction of events. Thus, the study has outlined how one institution, through the transmission of cultural values in a new setting, has led in time to the altering of another institution, developed for other purposes in a fundamentally different historical setting.

At the end of this analysis, what emerges most clearly is the interdependence of values and social structures, and the variety of ways in which they can affect one another, both by design and without intent, both consciously and unknowingly.

It also seems that by considering the relationship between two or more sets of institutions rather than by focusing on the operating of one structure alone, it may be possible to come to a better understanding of the ways in which social change takes place than has hitherto been possible. Attention to a narrow aspect of social life has its roots in the desire to isolate one particular factor in order to assess its influence. While this clearly has many advantages, it would appear that there is a good case at the moment for what has been termed inter-institutional analysis, so that groups may be seen in their social context.

Social Change and Disorganization

In sociological research and theory there has always been a stress upon the breakdown of relationships in particular environments, and the social consequences of such phenomena. Durkheim's analysis of suicide[1] has led to the formulation of many theories which seek to explain the ways in which people may find themselves at a loss when the familiar relationships of the primary group are dissolved as a

---

1. E. Durkheim, *Suicide* (Translated by J. A. Spaulding and G. Simpson), London, 1952.

result of social change. In this country, it is in the field of housing policies that attention has been focused on these issues. It seemed at first that *anomie* often resulted when neighbourhood and kinship ties had broken down. Recent research, building on the findings of these earlier surveys, has been able to reach more sophisticated conclusions; the loss of kinship and local links does not necessarily lead to social disorganization for whole sections of society. The findings of this present research also indicate that rapid social change, including the disruption of friendship ties with earlier class mates and all the other factors associated with the processes of social mobility, need not create feelings of insecurity. The fact that the parish was no longer a primary group for the majority of the young people interviewed did not mean that they suffered from a sense of loneliness or purposelessness. On the contrary, they have shed with ease the old ties which held earlier generations together in the parochial community. Their education has given them new attitudes and ways of behaving which they find more acceptable and more meaningful in terms of their experiences as young men and women in contemporary society than those communicated to earlier generations through the parochial schools. The feelings of solidarity with other Catholics of a similar education involve the former pupils in a close network of relationships, preventing them from feeling uprooted; and they find this situation much more satisfying than formally constituted groups. They recognize the differences which have occurred between generations, between parishioners, but consider that they have gained rather than lost in the process. Yet these new relationships and structures have not arisen as the result of an all-embracing policy, but in a variety of ways, as individuals have associated together in informal groups by trial and error, rather than in conscious attempts to meet specific needs.

The research, therefore, reveals how unwise it is to assume that social disorganization automatically results from rapid social change. In the present situation, there have been abrupt changes in the social class hierarchy, but the strength of the structures and functions which have arisen round the schools have meant that there has been a rearrangement rather than a disorganization of relationships. The breakdown of ties with the neighbourhood community is not in itself a bad thing nor one which is inimical to the development of social relationships. Other ties arise and may in the long run prove more valuable to the individuals concerned than those by which they might otherwise have regulated their lives. One cannot preserve local communities out of sentiment; nor can one assume people always wish to retain them.[1]

1. Vereker and Mays, *op. cit.*, p. 81 *et seq.*

Consequences for the Religious Life

And what of the consequences for the religious life? It is no part of the role of the sociologist to examine the value of changes such as those which have been described in this book. But it does seem worthwhile pointing out some of the implications of this research. It seems that many traditional values have endured through higher education; indeed, they may become increasingly meaningful rather than the reverse. But at the same time, it appears that the religious structures which were designed for the purpose of developing and supporting those values no longer do so for some people. It could be argued that the potential religious life will only be realized for such people to the full if new institutionalized forms are devised to contain it.

It might also be suggested that at the present time there is too much stress upon preserving the traditional structures for their own sakes without sufficient understanding of their aims. Socio-religious institutions and groupings such as parochial associations are not ends in themselves, yet lack of understanding of this can lead to utopian proposals for further developments which are virtually impossible in contemporary society. Parishes came into being so that certain beliefs and values about the nature of social life could find a means of expression in a context readily intelligible to the faithful. While the neighbourhood community was a social reality, such an ideal was possible in the parish. When, however, as at the present time, local ties are speedily disappearing, such a concept of social life is much less meaningful. As a result, far from supporting the discharge of spiritual and social responsibilities, it may have the opposite effect; for the faithful may react against such a setting so strongly that even the social community of the Church Herself may be rejected.

It has been shown that it is the way in which the social systems of the grammar schools operate rather than individual wishes which prevent their pupils from participating in the life of the parish. Where can such people fit into the institutionalized life of the Church as it now exists? A few manage to return to the parish because their families or former class mates provide a bridge; others are determined to find their feet in extra-parochial groups. But these are the few. The process of attending grammar schools has detached the majority from their parishes both psychologically as individuals and socially as a section of people. They are effectually removed by the channel of the school out of the path of the parish, yet expected later in life to be reintegrated into it. It would, of course, be possible to suggest ways in which the former pupils of grammar schools might be drawn back into the parish. An obvious way, for instance, would be for the schools to change their policies regarding religious organizations; pupils could be encouraged to belong to such associations in a parochial setting.

But would there be much value in this? How would their religious needs be met within the parochial structure as it now exists? Some of these needs have been discovered in this inquiry; more remain to be considered through later investigations. Respondents' answers reveal the problems they themselves reported experiencing, especially the difficulty of living as Christians in a *milieu* which they regarded as often hostile to their beliefs and values. That they felt they also needed support in maintaining their values was clear from their attitudes towards one another, and their stress upon the necessity of being in contact with others of similar views. Up to now the peer group has met this need. But how long will this group hold them? What will happen as more get married, others move away from the city, and new patterns of living are introduced into their lives? There are indications already that this sub-culture is able to hold only those who conform to 'the middle of the road', staying in the Liverpool environment and taking employment within a certain range of professions; it is possible that the group will not be able in the future to hold the more adventurous socially and intellectually.

Moreover, it can be asked if this peer group, which may tend to isolate the members from the wider community in which they live, has much religious significance. It has already been said that often those who were interviewed made it plain that activities which were organized by Catholic groups did not always strike them as being distinctive from the point of view of religion. In the development of this sub-culture, it would seem that it is often the cultural rather than the religious aspects of Catholicism which are the binding force. One can almost be said to 'belong' merely because one is 'that sort of person'. For it must be stressed that it was a common educational experience, and not religious worship, which was the mainspring of this kind of attachment. The validity of this point can be seen in the rejection from intimate friendship of fellow parishioners who had not shared their education at grammar schools. One might at first sight describe the ties between the former pupils of Liverpool Catholic grammar schools as religious bonds, but on closer examination it seems much more probable that it was a common cultural background which fostered their growth. True, it is values which had made them conscious of shared ideas and ways of thinking and behaving. But it remains for further investigation to distinguish more plainly how far these can be described as religious values, and how far they can be traced to cultural and class ideologies transmitted through the schools.

C.A.S.—12

These questions need to be examined carefully before suggestions are put forward. On the basis of the total lack of interest most felt for the parish, the writer can only conclude that the view that they will later return to the parish, for instance, on marriage, is too optimistic. People's ideas and ways of thinking do not suddenly change overnight simply because they enter a new state of life. The indifference of the former pupils of grammar schools towards the parish was so radical, so much a part of them, that there does not seem to be much basis for the expectation that the majority will later see it in a new light.

These young Catholics also referred to the need to face contemporary problems with a religious knowledge more fitted to maturity than that of an adolescent. They volunteered the information that as individuals they had failed to meet this situation. How can this need be satisfied within the context of the ordinary Liverpool parish? The duty of the priest to give religious instruction is clearly one which obliges him to reach the ordinary members of the congregation, not the odd handful. The policy some Catholics have developed for themselves of choosing another church, such as the Cathedral, may enable them to develop a fuller understanding of their faith than listening to the sermons in their own parishes.

Having said all this, there is another question to be asked: just how acceptable would such people really be in the parish as it now exists? They are different in their outlook from earlier generations of Catholics. They would probably chafe at certain demands, and find it difficult to accept the priest's decisions. They are used to situations, at the university for example, where lay initiative is demanded. What place would such people have in the parochial structure as it now stands? Is it not perhaps a case of distance lending enchantment?

This does not in any way imply a plea for the abolition of traditional structures, (even if this was remotely feasible at the present time), nor yet the tacit withdrawal of emphasis upon the parish: but rather it suggests that in contemporary society there are new religious and social needs which cannot always be met by structures which were developed out of the needs of earlier generations. It is perhaps time that such traditional groupings were complemented by new kinds of adaptation to change, as has been the case with the establishment and development of the University Catholic Societies. For the views and behaviour of young Catholics at this period are radically different from those which were once prevalent. The new generation of the Church in the city is now composed, on the one hand, of growing numbers of people who are becoming socially mobile, many of them reaching universities and the higher professions; for these people, the ties to the neighbourhood which made the parish a social community have little or no meaning. They have views which they are ordinarily capable of expressing for themselves and they seek guidance from the clergy in spiritual matters alone. And on the other hand, there are the far greater numbers of young people from secondary modern schools (fewer of the new ones being parochial, be it remembered, with the advent of the inter-parochial schools) who have not yet grown to reject the parish completely; but they have learned to look for what it may well not be the function of the parish to provide.

The findings of this study reveal how this new generation of Catholics in Liverpool has not grasped any sense of the parish's importance. The wider social community of the parish has been dismissed as unimportant by the grammar school people, and rejected in favour of primary group relations with one another. On the other hand, the answers of the young people from St. Henry's school show how confused they have become as to what the parish is; to them it is an institution which ought to provide them with a youth club, one without religious connotations, they stress. The fact that emphasis has been placed in this inquiry upon the former pupils of grammar schools does not indicate a lack of interest in the attitudes and ways of thinking of the far greater numbers of young Catholics who attend secondary modern schools. Their views and behaviour which were touched upon in Chapter 11 need to be examined very carefully, especially now that more and more Catholic secondary modern schools are on an inter-parochial basis. The implications such a policy will have for the parochial structure are clearly tremendous.

It seems worthwhile touching upon another aspect of the religious life at this point. The question of religious education in general is a source of growing disquiet at the present time, and the methods and syllabuses of the religious bodies have come under fire, with some justification. The extent to which university chaplains of various denominations report the distress felt by students at the loss of their faith is but one indication of how inadequate has been the kind of religious teaching which leaves the young person unable to visualize belief as developing as the individual matures, rather than as a set of ideas learned at an early age and having relevance to that period of life alone.

These findings have revealed to some extent the ideas which a section of educated young people have received about the nature of the Church, a question which is of particular importance at the moment.[1] It need hardly be said that there is considerable room for

1. See the reports of the discussions of the schema *De Ecclesia* in the Second Vatican Council, 1962, as, for instance, in *Informations Catholiques Internationales*, 1. February, 1963. For an interesting general account of the debate see Xavier Rynne, *Letters from Vatican City*, London, 1963.

C.A.S.—12*

examining the methods of religious instruction which have resulted
not only in defensive, and even hostile, attitudes towards the wider
society, but in a concept of Christianity as little more than a set of
spiritual beliefs, of faith as something to be 'kept', and a view of the
social life of the Church identified with outdated parochial associations. It seems highly probable that many of these ideas can be
traced not only to the social history of the Catholic Church in
England, but also to the nature of the religious teaching in grammar
schools, especially in the later years, which is still profoundly influenced by Counter-Reformation debates. It would be hard to find
teachings less adapted to the climate of our times, when so many
people are anxious to break down traditional enmities which have
little rational basis; often those who were interviewed reported how
inadequate they found the religious teaching which they had received
in the Sixth Form.

To dismiss all the schools' doctrinal teaching on the basis of
views expressed by former pupils in after life would be obviously
unjust. But it does seem that there is a great need to re-examine the
content of the religious instruction given to young people, in the light
of the kinds of experiences which they are likely to encounter now,
rather than to be concerned with facing the problems of previous
generations. At a period when attitudes towards religious structures
are changing with remarkable and perhaps unparalleled, speed, it is
all the more important that the nature of the Church should be
clearly grasped, so that vital developments in the religious life will
not be impeded.

Relevance of the Research

An obvious question at the end of this investigation is, why should
the ideas and affairs of such a small section of society matter? Are
the results of anything more than a cursory academic interest?

Were the basic situation described here true of only one small
region, it could be said that there is little point in considering it.
Certainly, to speak in terms of institutional adaptation to change
would seem too thrusting. But much of what is taking place in
Liverpool today is happening throughout the world. To consider,
first of all, only one of the terms of reference used in this research,
members of the Catholic Church throughout the world are experiencing the emergence from poverty that leads through the solid ranks of
the working classes, to the higher professions. They are no longer
homogeneous populations, and it cannot be said that their needs
can be met in one way only. As the first chapter showed in discussing
what work has already been done, remarkably little is known about
the results of such developments. Studies of attitudes indicate that

educated Catholics tend to accept the beliefs of Catholicism; censuses of Mass attendance show that the better a Catholic's standard of education, the more likely he is to fulfil his obligation to attend church. But if one can perhaps infer a possible relationship between values and behaviour on the basis of these two pieces of evidence, it is as much as can be said. Little is known of the way in which ordinary social relationships are influenced by values, nor how those who are becoming socially mobile live as Christians in an urban society, nor what the ultimate outcome of it all is likely to be.

These questions require attention through a detailed consideration in depth of small sections of people, and this investigation has shown how much co-operation can be obtained in such an inquiry. The particular interest of the Liverpool situation lies in the fact that it is possible to see in one generation changes which have taken place more slowly elsewhere. Just as one can gain insight into ordinary questions of adjustment and assimilation through the extreme problems of adaptation encountered by immigrants, so here it is possible to grasp the salient aspects of change more easily.

What is happening at the moment in Liverpool has already taken place in many other regions of the country, and, indeed, of the world. While features such as the close contacts with fellow Catholics may be revealed in later inquiries to be only a local phenomenon, it seems likely that some factors discovered in this inquiry are true of the Catholic middle classes in general. The trend towards the acceptance of ideas and attitudes of the wider society, particularly in the fields of education and social class, is an indication of how a different cultural expression of Catholicism emerges. By studying the attitudes and behaviour of a small section of people in a social context, this investigation has tried to overcome some of the limitations of superficial descriptions and explanations of trends in religious groups.

The young Catholics described in this study might be termed members of a transitional society. In the circumstances, the growing pains of confusion and tension are only to be expected. It is the next move which is the crucial one. A policy has been set on foot to accelerate the processes of social mobility in Britain today. It has been accepted by the Catholic Church, and the movement of Catholics to the middle classes has been fostered. It remains to be seen how the consequences will be dealt with in the future. Might not a preliminary step in adapting to the changing social situation be the better understanding of the behaviour and ways of thinking of those living in it, and in particular of their needs and potentialities in an industrialized society?

From the point of view of higher education, too, it must be pointed out that when attempts are being made to improve or reform an educational system, we need to discover the consequences of particular forms of schooling not only for the individuals and their families who experience them, but also for society as a whole. The kinds of views and opinions communicated through each type of school have repercussions for the community in general, since education influences the part people will take in social life and the attitudes they will have towards it.

But at the end, it must be said that some of the issues discussed here have a considerably wider relevance.The discovery of the problems which new administrative decisions introduce has been left largely to chance, almost on the principle of 'What we don't know, we don't bother about'. The administrator is commonly confronted with people's values in relation to his policies, and his sensitivity to beliefs may well be the crucial factor in the success of his work. Knowledge of how social situations are brought about, and of the values and ideas which may change relationships and institutions, is essential if social progress is to be stimulated and achieved, instead of simply a way made clear for change. It cannot be said too often that the description and prediction of social trends do not reveal the inevitable future. Rather, they indicate what is happening, and what may happen, so that intelligent decisions may be made to plan what *will* happen. This investigation has already shown how deliberately planned change has taken place. Its effects can, and indeed must, be coped with in precisely the same rational manner.

Policies such as the educational and religious which are central to this study represent not only the desire to improve social conditions, but also the willingness to accept the responsibility of translating ideas into action. The fact that the results may not always be those which were expected or sought should not deter us from recognizing and respecting the principles underlying such administrative decisions. The sociologist is confronted with the challenge to apply himself with industry and responsibility to the discovery of the social and other consequences of change, not merely because of the intrinsic and theoretical interest of the situations, but also because such a step may be the preliminary to the formulation of far-seeing policies and their application in the future.

This research was planned and executed against a background of rapidly changing attitudes towards religious beliefs and institutions, both inside and outside of Christianity. In presenting the findings and the implications as seen by the author, it is hoped that the results may be thought to indicate that sociological research involves not only observation and analysis, but also the making of a positive contribution to the development of the social environment which stimulated it.

APPENDIX

The following is a copy of the schedule used to interview the former pupils of Catholic Grammar Schools.[1]

INTERVIEW SCHEDULE

Schedule Number: Place of interview:

Sex: Date:

                            Time:

SECTION I. FAMILY

1. Date of birth:
2. Address:
3. How long have you lived at this address?
4. Where did you live before that?
5. Have you ever lived anywhere else?
6a. Family Structure:

CHRISTIAN NAME	RELATION	SEX	AGE	MARITAL STATUS	OCCUPATION	LAST SCHOOL	SAME ADDRESS

6b. Do you know how long your family has lived in Liverpool?
7. Do you know where your family came from before that?

SECTION II. OCCUPATIONAL AND EDUCATIONAL EXPERIENCES

8. Occupation, or place and type of study?
9. Occupational or educational history since leaving school (excluding vacation work):
10. Which school did you last attend?
11. How long were you there?
12. Which school did you attend before that: Dates?
13. What sort of school was it?
                        Parochial,
                        Private R.C.,
                        Private non-R.C.,
                        L.A. primary,
                        Other.

[1] This is not laid out in the form of the schedule.

14a. Have you ever been to any other school?
14b. Which one?
14c. Dates:
15a. Do you see regularly any of the people you went to the grammar school with?
15b. On what occasions?
16. Does the grammar school have a former pupil's association?
17. What sort of activities does it have?
18. Do you belong to it?
19. If yes, how did you come to join?
20. If yes, how often do you go?
21a. If no association, would you like the school to have one?
21b. Why?
22. If no association, what sort of activities would you like such an organization to provide?
23. If an association, what do you think of its activities?
24. If a member, are there any new activities that you would like it to have?
25. If not a member, have you any particular reason for not belonging?
26. What do you think is the purpose of such organizations?
27. Do you think this is a useful purpose?
28. Do you ever go back to your grammar school? On what occasions? How often?
29. Do you go for any special reason?
30a. Do you ever see any of the people you went to your previous school/s with?
30b. On what occasions?
30c. Where?
30d. How often?

SECTION IIII. SCHOOL ORGANIZATIONS

31. Were there any organizations or clubs functioning in the grammar school while you were a pupil?
32a. Did you belong to any of them?
32b. Which ones?
33. What sort of activities did they have?
34. What did you think of them?
35. Were there any religious organizations in your grammar school?
36. Was membership optional?
37a. Did you belong to any of them?
37b. Dates?
38. Did you hold any office?
39. What did you think of these religious organizations?
40. Do you now belong to any of them?
41a. If yes, have you any particular reason for remaining a member?
41b. If no, did you have any particular reason for leaving?
42. Were there any religious organizations in the school/s you attended before going to the grammar school?
43. What did you think of them?
44. Was membership optional?
45a. Did you belong to any of them?
45b. Dates?
46. Do you still belong to any of them?
47a. If yes, have you any special reason for remaining?
47b. If no, did you have any special reason for leaving?

SECTION IV. SIXTH FORM ACTIVITIES

48. Did you have any particular reason for staying on to the Sixth Form?
49a. Do you think it was worthwhile staying on to the Sixth Form?
49b. In what ways?

50. What do you think of the discipline prevailing in the Sixth Form?
51a. Do you think you were given any responsibility in the Sixth Form?
51b. In what ways?
52. Did you hold any position of particular responsibility in the Sixth Form?
53. Do you think there were any ways in which the situation could have been improved?
54. What subjects did you take in the Sixth Form?
55. How often did you receive religious instruction in the Sixth Form?
56. What would you say were the main ideas covered in these lessons?
57. Did you use any special books for these religious lessons?
58. Did you take the Higher Religious Certificate?
59. Who took the religious lessons?
60. Did this teacher take any other lessons?
61. Did the religious lessons interest you as much as lessons in other subjects?
62. Have you any criticisms to make about these religious lessons?
63. Would you suggest any changes in the Sixth Form religious programme?
64. What would you say was the general attitude in your class towards these lessons?
65a. Do you think that people change their ideas about religion after leaving school?
65b. In what ways?
66a. Do you think you have yourself?
66b. In what ways?
67a. Do you think Catholics have any need to study their religion after leaving school?
67b. Why?
67c. On what lines?
67d. How?
68. What in your experience are the main reasons why some Catholics stop going to Church?

SECTION V. CHAPLAIN AND SERVICES

69a. Did your grammar school have a Chaplain?
69b. Who was he?
69c. Where did he come from?
70. Did he ever give any classes in religion?
71. Were there any opportunities when you could have spoken to the Chaplain personally if you wished?
72. Was there anyone else to provide advice if you wanted it?
73. How often did you have prayers in school?
74. What did you think about prayers at assembly?
75a. Were there any religious services, other than assembly, held regularly in school?
75b. Who conducted them?
75c. Where were they held?
76. What did you think of them?
77a. Were there any religious services held on special occasions? e.g. Retreats.
77b. Who conducted them?
77c. Where were they held?
78. What did you think of them?
79a. Did any priest ever come to the school you attended before going to a grammar school?
79b. Who was he and where did he come from?
80. How often did he come?
81a. Did you ever see him after you left the school?
81b. When and where?
82a. Do you ever wish you had gone to a different school from ....?
82b. Why?
82c. If so, what sort of school do you wish you had gone to?

SECTION VI. LEISURE TIME ACTIVITIES

83. What were your main spare time interests while you were at school?
84. Who were your special friends while you were at school?

	a	b	c	d	e	f	g
CHRISTIAN NAME	ADDRESS	SEX	SCHOOL	AGE	SAME CLASS	RELATION	RELIGION

85. What are your main leisure time activities now?
86. Do you go round with any particular friend or group of friends now?
87. Where do you meet them?
88. Do you know their occupations and religion?
89. Do you know which schools they last attended?
90a. Do you belong to any clubs or organizations? e.g. political? youth clubs?
90b. Where?
91. How often do you go?
92. How long have you belonged?
93. How did you come to join?
94. What do you think of ....?
95. Do you hold any office?
96. Have you belonged to any others in the past?
97. When did you leave?
98. Did you have any special reason for leaving?

SECTION VII. PAROCHIAL ACTIVITIES

99.   In which parish do you live?
100. How long have you lived in this parish?
101. What activities are there in the parish, apart from the services in church?
102. Do you know who runs these activities?
103. What do you think of these activities?
104a. Do any of your family ever take part in them?
104b. In which ones?
105. Have they ever done so in the past?
106a. Do you yourself take any part in them?
106b. In which ones?
107. What does taking part involve?
108. If so, how did you come to do so?
109. How long have you taken part?
110. If yes, do you go with anyone to ....?
111. If yes, do you ever meet any of the regular attenders elsewhere?
112. Are there any activities in the parish in which you have taken part in the past, and in which you no longer do so?
113. Did you have any particular reason for leaving?
114a. Were you ever an altar server?
114b. Dates?
114c. Where?
114d. If no longer, did you have a special reason for leaving?

115a. Were you ever in the parish choir?
115b. If no longer, did you have any special reason for leaving?
115c. Dates?
116. What did your teachers think about your taking part in parish activities while you were at school?
117. What do you think about the organization of your parish?
118. Are there any activities which you would like to see in your parish, which are not there already?
119. How many priests are there in your parish?
120a. Do you ever see any of the priests from your parish?
120b. On what occasions?
120c. How often?
121. How often do the priests visit the homes of the parishioners in your parish?
122a. If moved, did you take part in any of the activities in the other parish?
122b. Which ones?
122c. Dates:
123. Do you still do so?
124a. Did any of your family ever take part?
124b. In which ones?
125. Do they still do so?
126a. In which of the two parishes would you prefer to live?
126b. Why?
127. What activities do you think should be provided in the ideal parish?

SECTION VIII. EXTRA-PAROCHIAL ACTIVITIES

128. Do you ever take any part in any Catholic activities outside the parish?
129. How did you first come to do so?
130. What do you think about these activities?
131. Do you usually go with any one to ....?
132. Have you ever taken part in any other Catholic activities in the past? When and where?
133. What did you think of them?
134. Did you have any special reason for leaving?

SECTION IX. IF AT UNIVERSITY

135. Do you take part in any University activities apart from the lectures?
136. Do you belong to any associations or organizations at University?
137. Is there a University Catholic Society?
138. Do you know anything about it?
139. How did you find out about it?
140. What activities does it have?
141a. Do you ever take part in any of its activities?
141b. In which ones?
142a. What do you think about these activities?
142b. Have you any criticisms to make?
143. How did you first come to take part in these activities?
144a. If no, have you ever been invited to do so?
144b. In what way?
145. Have you any special reason for not taking part?
146a. Have you ever done so in the past?
146b. When?
147. If yes, how often do you take part?
148. What do you think is the purpose of a University Catholic Society?
149. Do you think this is a useful purpose?
150. What sort of activities do you think a University Catholic Society should provide?
151. Do you know any Catholics at University?
152. Where did you meet them?
153. Do they take part in any of the activities of the Catholic Society?

154. What do you think are the main reasons why they do (not)?
155a. Do you ever see the University Chaplain?
155b. On what occasions?
156. Have any of your family been to a University?

SECTION X. IF AT A CATHOLIC TRAINING COLLEGE

157. Are/were there any Catholic organizations at College?
158. Is/was membership optional?
159. Do/did you belong to any of them?
160. Do/did you hold any office?
161. What does/did this membership involve?
162. How did you come to join?
163. What do you think about these organizations?
164a. Do you think you will continue to be a member after leaving College?
164b. Are you still a member?
164c. If not, when did you leave?
165. Why?
166a. Is/was there a Chaplain at College?
166b. Who?
167a. How often do/did you see him?
167b. On what occasions?

NOTES

Reaction of respondent to interviewer.
General remarks regarding the study.
If at respondent's home, comments on other members of the family met.
Other remarks.

INDEX OF AUTHORS

INDEX OF SUBJECTS